D1422915

500

vegan dishes

500

vegan dishes

Deborah Gray

Inspiring | Educating | Creating | Entertaining

First published in the UK in 2011 by
Apple Press, an imprint of The Quarto Group
The Old Brewery,
6 Blundell Street,
London,
N7 9BH,
United Kingdom
Tel (0)20 7700 6700 Fax (0)20 7700 8066
www.QuartoKnows.com

ISBN: 978-1-84543-416-8
QTT.FHV

This book was conceived, designed and produced by
Quintet, an imprint of The Quarto Group
58 West Street,
Brighton,
West Sussex,
BN1 2RA,
United Kingdom

Food Stylist: Valentina Harris
Photographer: Ian Garlick
Art Director: Michael Charles
Editorial Assistant: Holly Willsher
Managing Editor: Donna Gregory
Publisher: Mark Searle

11

Printed in China by 1010 Printing International Ltd.

contents

introduction

Vegan food avoids all animal products including meat, dairy produce, eggs and animal-derived products such as gelatin and honey. It is essentially a plant-based diet consisting of grains, beans, lentils, nuts, seeds, vegetables and fruits. Millions of people worldwide are vegans.

Why eat a vegan diet? A vegan diet is healthy, low in fat, high in fibre and rich in vitamins, minerals and antioxidants. Vegans tend to eat more whole grains and are less dependent on processed foods. Therefore, as long as the diet is varied, the vegan diet is the healthiest option of all. There is evidence to suggest that eating a vegan diet may reduce the risk of developing some cancers, diabetes, obesity, heart disease and several other major diseases. Vegans, however, can become deficient in vitamin B12, iodine, selenium, omega-3 and vitamin D2, so it is essential to ensure that this is taken into consideration when planning a menu. Many feel that a specially designed vitamin and mineral supplement is helpful.

A vegan diet is also more sustainable. Animals raised for consumption use more protein, water and calories than they produce, so eating a plant-based diet is a great way to reduce an individual's carbon footprint. Globally, livestock farms are continuing to be a cause of deforestation and are huge consumers of increasingly scarce water supplies. Livestock are also responsible for 18% of the world's total carbon emissions. With the planet's population increasing, there is a strong argument that a vegan diet is the only way forward. Many vegans are also motivated by compassion for animals. They object to the exploitation of animals, the conditions in which they are raised and the idea of killing animals for human use.

It may seem difficult to integrate a vegan diet into a standard meat-eating family diet. Many of the recipes in this book are familiar, however, and have been adapted to become vegan-friendly. By following the general principles of vegan cuisine, it is surprising how many favourite recipes can be modified to suit all tastes. In fact, the substitution may well go unnoticed by all but the most discerning of family members. In general, this book has avoided the use of processed vegan 'meats', but they are widely available in supermarkets as well as in specialised health food shops. For the widest variety of specialised foods, try using one of the Internet-based health shops, which will ship an impressive range of goods to your door.

ingredients

The following is a practical guide to some vegan ingredients that may be less familiar than vegetables and herbs.

agar agar
A sea vegetable-based gelatin substitute that can be used for thickening and gelling.

agave syrup
A very sweet syrup made from the juices of the Mexican blue agave plant. Use it as a sugar or honey substitute; 250 ml (8 fl oz) agave nectar is equal to 175 g (6 oz) sugar. If substituting agave nectar in a baked dish, reduce the liquid in the dish by a third.

beans
Beans have been a vital source of protein since ancient times. They are also high in fibre and complex carbohydrates. Being inexpensive and versatile, it is no wonder that they are central to the vegan diet. A wide variety of beans are available fresh, dried or tinned. As a rough guide, 500 g (1 lb 2 oz) of dried beans produces three and a half 400-g (14-oz) tins of beans. To cook dried beans, pick over the beans and remove any damaged ones. Soak the beans in cold water overnight or for at least 4 hours, prior to cooking, both to reduce cooking time and to aid digestion. Drain the soaked beans and place them in a saucepan and cover with water or stock (the liquid should be about 5 cm (2 in) above the top of the beans). Do not salt until the beans are cooked, because the salt will toughen them during cooking. Bring to a fast boil for 5 minutes (10 for kidney beans to remove toxins), then simmer over a low heat until tender (see chart below). It is impossible to state cooking times precisely; therefore, cooking several types of beans together is best avoided.

The following are the most commonly cooked dried beans:

Bean type	Cooking time
Mung beans Split peas	35–45 minutes
Dried peas Dried broad beans Butterbeans	45 minutes to $1\frac{1}{4}$ hours
Cannellini beans Bortolini beans Kidney beans	$1\frac{1}{4}$–$1\frac{3}{4}$ hours
Adzuki beans	1–$1\frac{1}{2}$ hours
Black beans Chickpeas Haricot beans Pinto beans	$1\frac{1}{2}$–2 hours
Soyabeans	2–3 hours

brown rice syrup
A mild, lightly refined syrup that contains complex sugars, which are absorbed slowly in the bloodstream. Use it as a sugar or honey substitute; 250 ml (8 fl oz) brown rice syrup is equal to 225 g (8 oz) sugar. If substituting it in a baked dish, reduce the liquid in the dish by one third. Note that some brands are made with barley enzymes, so they are not gluten-free.

carob
A chocolate-like substance made from the pod of the carob tree. It comes in powder, chips or in a bar. Carob beans are also the source of locust bean gum.

cheese

A number of manufacturers make soya-based cheese substitutes in a variety of flavours and textures. These include hard cheeses, such as cheddar and Parmesan, mozzarella and soft cream cheeses. In general, they have the same cooking and melting qualities as those cheeses they are mimicking. These non-dairy cheeses are available in health food shops and over the Internet. (See also nutritional yeast, page 12, and cheese substitutes, page 19.)

egg replacer

A commercially available blend of starches and leavening agents that can be used in place of eggs in many recipes. (See also egg substitutes, pages 20–21.)

fats

The following fats are acceptable in a vegan diet: soya or other non-dairy margarine, non-dairy butter, non-dairy spreads, non-hydrogenated white vegetable fat and nut butters. (See also butter substitutes, page 18, and oils, pages 12–13.)

flour

Wheat flour is used throughout this book, unless otherwise stated. The following flours are wheat-and-gluten-free: arrowroot, brown rice, buckwheat, cornflour, chickpea (gram flour), cornmeal, millet, potato, rice, sorghum, soya and tapioca flour. They may require the addition of slightly more liquid than wheat flours, so always check package details.

grains

These include barley, buckwheat (kasha) corn, kamut, millet, oats, quinoa, rice, rye, spelt and whole-wheat grains. They form the backbone of the vegan diets and are either cooked whole or as a flour. To cook them whole, place in lightly salted boiling water, reduce the heat to a simmer and cook until tender. Cooking time can take from 15 minutes for rice to 2 hours.

honey

Honey is an animal-derived product and as such is not vegan. There are several good syrup substitution options, including agave, brown rice, golden, fruit and maple syrups. The different syrups have very different sugar levels per teaspoon, so check the labels.

lentils

Lentils are legumes. They are low in fat and high in protein and fibre, and they are a vegan staple. Red, green and brown lentils are the most commonly used, but Asian markets and health shops offer a wider range. Always pick over lentils to remove stray stones or broken lentils before cooking, then rinse in cold water.

To cook lentils, use 100 g (3¹/₂ oz) lentils to 375 ml (13 fl oz) water or stock. Add flavourings such as herbs, garlic and onions to the liquid in the pan, but do not add salt until the lentils are soft. Bring the liquid to a boil, add the lentils, boil rapidly for 2–3 minutes, then simmer until tender. Cooking time varies from about 15 minutes for red lentils to about 20–25 minutes for other types. If using lentils in salads, drain as soon as they are tender; for purées, soups, and stews, a slightly softer texture is better.

Brown lentils	Plumper than green lentils, can become mushy if overcooked, good for soups
French green lentils (puy lentils)	Retain their shape after cooking, good in salads and stews
Green lentils	A large flat lentil that holds its shape well, good in soups and salads
Red lentils	Become mushy if overcooked, good in soups, stews and purées

maple syrup

Derived from the sap of the maple tree, maple syrup has a wonderful rich, tonal flavour. Do not confuse it with 'maple-flavoured' pancake syrups. In cooking, use 250 ml (8 fl oz) maple syrup for every 275 g (10 oz) sugar. Reduce liquid in baked recipes by a quarter.

mycoprotein

A low-fat, meat-free protein whose principle ingredient is a form of fungus. Beware, most varieties contain small quantities of egg, so they are not vegan.

nutritional yeast

Don't be put off by its fish food-like appearance. Nutritional yeast has a strong, almost cheese-like flavour and is great as a Parmesan cheese substitute. It also adds a depth of flavour to any soup or stew that is in need of a little oomph. Do not confuse it with brewer's yeast, as they are not the same thing. Purchase in health food shops or specialist food shops.

nuts

Nuts are a good source of protein and fibre. Almonds, cashew, macadamia, peanuts, pecans and walnuts are great store cupboard staples. Store in a cool, dark place or in the freezer.

oils

Extra-virgin olive oil has the best flavour and is a good choice where the flavour has a chance to shine through such as in stirfries and salads. However, where the oil facilitates cooking or in baking, subtle-flavoured oils such as sunflower, safflower or rapeseed oils are best. In general, avoid vegetable oil. This is usually hydrogenated, which results in higher trans fat levels (the bad cholesterols). Nut oils are great in gourmet cooking. Experiment with them in salad dressings or sprinkle them on freshly cooked vegetables. Peanut oil has gained in popularity and is particularly good for stirfrying because of its high heat tolerance.

Sesame oil is good for added flavour, especially in Asian dishes. Because of the chemistry of the oil, flax oil should not be used in cooking; however, it is high in omega-3 fatty acids and can be used in place of fish oils in the diet. Use it in place of butter on dishes such as popcorn and steamed vegetables.

filo pastry

This pastry dough is vegan and very low in fat, which makes it perfect for making quick and impressive pastries. It comes packaged, either fresh or frozen, in a bundle of sheets. It is best to defrost filo slowly, use it at room temperature and to work with it quickly, keeping the sheets covered with a clean damp cloth to prevent them from drying out.

seitan

Seitan is made from wheat gluten and is a good source of protein. It may be made at home by removing starch from glutinous wheat flour, but is more commonly purchased from the refrigerated section of the health food shop. Its resemblance to meat in both appearance and texture makes it a popular meat substitute. It is the basis for many-meat alternative products.

sugar

White sugar may or may not be vegan. It is made from both cane and beet sugar. Cane sugar is refined by filtering through charcoal; in some factories this may be derived from cow bones. Beet sugar does not require charcoal filtering as part of the refining process, so it is animal-free. Some vegans avoid commercial white sugar entirely by substituting raw sugar or unbleached cane sugar, available in health shops. Vegan organic, icing sugar is available but hard to find; however, you can make your own icing sugar by processing 500 g (1 lb 2 oz) granulated sugar with 2 tablespoons cornflour on high power in the food processor. Brown sugar may be refined or unrefined; its brown colouring is due to the presence of molasses. Demerara and muscavado are brown sugars derived from evaporated cane juice, so they avoid the filtering process.

tempeh

Tempeh is fermented soya bean cake. It may be marinated, fried, grilled or baked. It can also be crumbled and used as a minced meat substitute in dishes such as chilli.

texturised vegetable protein (TVP)

TVP is made from defatted soya flour, a by-product of the extraction of soya bean oil, hence it is also known as soya protein. It is high in protein but low in fat. TVP comes in small dry chunks resembling dried vegetables or in a ground form. Because of its varying texture and its flavourless quality, TVP is manufactured to mimic meat in the form of minced beef and chicken fillets, for instance. It is often used in chilli, tacos, veggie burgers, stews, curries and soups.

tofu

Tofu is a soya bean curd available in several textures and an increasing number of flavours. Being high in protein, it is a staple of a vegan diet. Firm and extra-firm tofu hold their shape, absorb flavours well and can be chopped or cut into slices, then fried, grilled or baked. Place in a colander on top of a bowl, cover the tofu with a plate and weigh down with a tin or similar weight. Leave for a minimum of 20 minutes or overnight. Tofu may be frozen to alter its texture. The result is a chewier more 'meaty' tofu with a sponginess that enables it to soak up more flavour when marinated. Defrost completely before use. Silken or soft tofu has a custard-like texture and a mild creamy flavour. It is excellent in desserts, sauces, dressings and as an addition to soups and stews.

yoghurt

Soya yoghurt is available plain and in a range of flavours. The brands vary in taste and texture, so test the market for your favourite.

animal-free substitutes

There are a number of options for substituting non-vegan products in the diet.

milk substitutes

The most commonly used non-dairy milk is soya milk, but oat milk, almond milk and rice milk are also easily available. All may be used in cooking and in beverages. Non-dairy milks are sold in the refrigerated section of most grocery shops and in non-refrigerated, boxed form on the shelves. Non-dairy milks are available in vanilla and chocolate flavours; always check the package to be sure the flavoured milk is vegan. Seek the advice of a health professional before using non-dairy milks for infants.

Almond milk: A lightly sweet milk good for cereals and in beverages. A good choice for cooking desserts or in baking. It contains high levels of vitamin A and other vitamins and minerals and omega fatty acids, but it is lower in protein than soya milk. Most are not soya-free because they use soya lecithin. It is free of cholesterol and saturated fat.

homemade almond milk

150 g (5 oz) raw almonds	**1 l (1¾ pt) water**
1 tbsp brown rice syrup	**pinch salt**

Blend the ingredients in a blender until creamy and smooth. Pour through a fine mesh bag or a muslin cloth into a bowl, squeezing the bag to force though all the liquid. Chill.
Makes 1 litre (1¾ pints)

Coconut milk: A sweet milk naturally found in the heart of the coconut. It is used in certain cuisines, such as Thai food and some desserts. Rarely available fresh, most varieties are made by squeezing the liquid out of coconut flesh and then adding water. It is high in saturated fats but low in calories and protein.

homemade coconut milk

125 g (4 oz) shredded coconut   **750 ml (1⅓ pt) hot (not boiling) water**

Combine the coconut and water in a bowl; cool to room temperature. Pour through a fine mesh bag or muslin cloth into a bowl, squeezing the bag to force though all the liquid. Chill. *Makes 625 ml (1 pint)*

Oat milk: Of the non-dairy milks, oat milk performs best at higher temperatures, especially in soups and stews where it will reduce and thicken slightly. It is cholesterol-free. Note that not all brands are gluten-free.

homemade oat milk

75 g (3 oz) porridge oats (not quick-cooking)   **1 tsp cornflour**
1.25 l (2 pt) water   **1 tbsp raw sugar**
1 tsp vanilla essence   **pinch salt**
pinch ground nutmeg

Combine the ingredients in a pan. Bring to the boil over medium-high heat, reduce the heat, cover and simmer until the oats are well cooked, approximately 10 minutes. Cool, then place in a blender and blend until smooth; allow to stand for 1 hour. Pour through a fine mesh bag or a muslin cloth into a bowl, squeezing the bag to force though all the liquid. Chill. *Makes 1 litre (1¾ pints)*

Rice milk: Thinner and sweeter than soya milk and higher in carbohydrates than cow's milk. It is also cholesterol-free and saturated fat-free. Rice milk is good on cereals and in beverages. It does not perform well in cooking without the use of stabilisers. Available fortified with calcium and vitamins A and D.

homemade rice milk
1 l (1¾ pt) water
½ tsp vanilla essence

100 g (4 oz) brown or white rice

Combine the ingredients in a pan. Bring to the boil over medium-high heat, reduce the heat, cover and simmer until the rice is very soft, about 25 minutes. Cool, then place in a blender and blend until smooth; allow to stand for 1 hour. Pour through a fine mesh bag or a muslin cloth into a bowl, squeezing the bag to force though all the liquid. Chill.
Makes 625 ml (1 pint)

Soya milk: Rich, higher in fat, fibre and protein than most non-dairy milks and probably the best milk substitute. It cooks well due to its stability at high temperatures. However, its taste is less successful in some delicate sweet dishes. It is cholesterol-free and saturated fat-free, but it has a high concentration of omega-3 fatty acids. It is commonly fortified with calcium.

cream substitutes
Soya cream is available on the supermarket shelves alongside soya milk. Nondairy sour cream is available in a more limited number of outlets and is found with the chilled foods. Mass market nondairy creamers are lactose-free but are not nondairy products because they tend to be made from casein, a protein-rich milk derivative. Look for soya-based creamers.

nondairy half-and-half
125 ml (4 fl oz) soya milk
2 tsp cornflour
1–2 tsp vanilla essence

65 g (2¼ oz) caster sugar
80 ml (3 fl oz) rapeseed oil

Place the soya milk, sugar and cornflour in a blender. Blend on a low speed and very, very slowly pour in the oil. Flavour with vanilla essence to taste. Chill until thickened.
Makes 250 ml (8 fl oz)

nondairy whipped cream
225 g (8 oz) firm tofu, drained
few drops vanilla essence

2 tsp brown rice syrup

Blend the ingredients in a blender until creamy and smooth.
Makes 250 ml (8 fl oz)

nondairy sour cream
350 g (12 oz) firm tofu, drained
2 tbsp lemon juice

90 ml (3 fl oz) rapeseed or sunflower oil
$^1/_2$ tsp salt

Blend the ingredients in a blender until creamy and smooth.
Makes 450 ml ($^3/_4$ pint)

butter substitutes

Margarine is the best substitute for butter, particularly in baking. However, not all commercial brands are vegan. Many contain whey or lactose and many contain unhealthy hydrogenated oils. Soya margarine is a sound choice, but in general, look for margarines that contain no trans fats or hydrogenated oils. Solid margarines (but not margarine spreads) can be successfully substituted for butter in most situations. White vegetable fat is the other alternative. This is a vegetable-based fat with a higher smoke point than margarine or butter, making it ideal for cooking at high temperatures, such as deep-frying. White vegetable fat is 100% fat, as opposed to margarine, which is typically 80%. This makes it good for use in pastry and shortbreads because the higher the fat content, the shorter or crumblier, the texture of the finished pastry. Solid fats also act as a leavening agent, helping cakes and scones to rise. Buttery spreads and soft margarines have a lower fat content than margarine or white vegetable fat, typically around 60%. Low-fat versions, however, may contain only 40% fat. The fat content will be on the packaging. These products are less successful for baking purposes, because the leavening, tenderising and crisping properties are reduced.

cheese substitutes

A wide variety of non-dairy cheese is available in health food and gourmet shops. Cheddar, mozzarella and soft cream cheese are relatively easy to find and should be cooked as their dairy counterparts. Non-dairy Parmesan is available too, but sprinkling a small quantity of nutritional yeast on food in place of Parmesan is a great substitute too. Some vegetarian cheeses may still contain small amounts of animal product using whey, rennet or casein, so always check that soya-based cheese substitutes are suitable for vegans.

mock parmesan

25 g (1 oz) nutritional yeast

40 g (1½ oz) sesame seeds, toasted

¼ tsp salt

Process the ingredients in a blender until completely ground. Note that some people prefer to use blanched almonds in place of sesame seeds.

Makes 65 g (2¼ oz)

nondairy cream cheese

40 g (1½ oz) raw cashews

225 g (8 oz) silken tofu, well drained

1–2 tbsp soya milk

1 tbsp brown rice or agave syrup

1 tsp salt

½ tsp white pepper

Place the cashews in boiling water; leave for at least 1 hour, then drain. Blend all the ingredients in a food processor until smooth. Taste and adjust the flavour, adding more salt or syrup depending on the end use. Refrigerate overnight, then use within 5 days.

Makes approximately 275 g (10 oz)

mayonnaise

Mayo is sometimes dairy-free anyway, but try making your own for a natural result.

nondairy mayonnaise

2 tbsp egg replacer

4 tbsp water

pinch salt

1¹/₂ tsp vinegar or lemon juice

1 tsp sugar

2 tsp dry mustard

125 ml (4 fl oz) sunflower oil

125 ml (4 fl oz) olive oil

In a blender or food processor, combine egg replacer and water and whisk with a fork until frothy. Add the salt, vinegar or lemon juice, sugar and the dry mustard, then blend on a low speed. Very, very slowly pour in the oils in a thin drizzle. Chill until thickened.

Makes about 375 ml (12 fl oz)

egg substitutes

A number of ingredients can be used in place of eggs depending on the function of the egg within the recipe. In general, eggs are used as a binder or as a rising agent. Tofu is a good substitute for eggs in dishes such as quiches or scrambled eggs or when eggs are required to bind. Silken tofu can be used in custards. For binding purposes, also try using tomato puree, mashed potatoes, cornflour or flour, mashed tofu or a little stock. For rising purposes, a commercial egg replacer, consisting of starches and leavening agents, can be bought in health shops. Follow the package directions for rehydration. You can also make an egg replacer at home in a large batch.

egg replacer

300 g (10 oz) ground arrowroot, tapioca starch or potato flour

65 g (2¹/₄ oz) baking powder

1 tbsp guar gum powder or xanthan gum powder

Combine the ingredients in an airtight container and shake vigorously to thoroughly mix. To replace 1 egg, combine 1½ teaspoons egg replacer, 1 tablespoon rapeseed oil and 2 tablespoons water. Whisk together until slightly frothy.

Makes 375 g (12¼ oz)

Component	Substitute
1 egg (binding, thickening, sweet)	50 g (2 oz) puréed prunes, unsweetened apple sauce or banana (+ ½ tsp baking powder in baked goods)
1 egg (binding, thickening, savoury)	65 g (2¼ oz) tomato purée, 50g (2 oz) mashed potato/squash or stock
1 egg (binding, limited leavening)	50 g (2 oz) beaten tofu
1 egg (leavening)	1 tbsp ground flax seed whisked in 3 tbsp hot water
1 egg (leavening)	2 tbsp water + 1 tbsp oil + 2 tsp baking powder
1 egg white (leavening)	1 tbsp plain agar agar dissolved in 1 tbsp water, whisked and chilled, then whisked again

basic recipes

There are a few recipes that every vegan cook needs to have on hand.

vegetable stock

Make vegetable stock from fresh vegetables or with scraps and peelings, avoiding root ends, dirty scrapings and starchy vegetables such as potatoes. Ensure a good mix of vegetables to avoid having a dominant flavour and try to have at least one carrot and one celery stick in the mix. A vegan staple, this stock freezes well.

500 g (1 lb 2 oz) mixed fresh vegetables,
   cleaned and roughly chopped
225 g (8 oz) onions, roughly chopped
2–4 garlic cloves, chopped

2 bay leaves
1 bunch fresh parsley
1/2 tsp each salt and whole peppercorns
2.25 l (4 pt) water

Place the vegetables in a pan with all the other ingredients. Bring to the boil over high heat. Reduce the heat and simmer, uncovered, for at least 1 hour – the stock should be reduced by about one half. Cool and strain. Use within 5 days or freeze.
Makes approximately 1.1 litres (2 pints)

vegan gravy

This is a flexible recipe. You may wish to add onion powder, herbs, tomato purée or a dash of wine, depending on what your gravy is to accompany.

500 ml (16 fl oz) vegetable stock (or water and
   a vegetable stock cube)
50 g (2 oz) flour
2 heaped tbsp nutritional yeast
1/2 tsp soya sauce

1/2 tsp Dijon mustard
1/2 tsp garlic powder
1 tbsp non-dairy margarine
sea salt and black pepper

In a small bowl, gradually mix the stock into the flour. Place in a saucepan with the nutritional yeast, soya sauce, mustard and garlic powder and slowly bring to a boil. Reduce the heat and stir in the non-dairy butter or margarine. Serve immediately or chill and reheat as required.

Makes 450 ml (1 pint)

tomato sauce

A classic recipe used as a base for many stews, pasta sauces and soups.

2 tbsp olive oil
1 medium onion, chopped
1 small carrot, shredded
2 garlic cloves, minced
1 400-g (14-oz) tin chopped tomatoes, drained

2 tbsp tomato purée
60 ml (2 fl oz) red wine or juice from
  the tomatoes
1 tsp dried basil or oregano
sea salt and black pepper

Heat the oil in a saucepan and add the onion and carrot. Cook gently over low heat until the onion is soft, 5 to 7 minutes. Add the garlic and cook for 1 minute, then stir in the remaining ingredients. Season to taste with salt and pepper. Cook for 10 minutes or until the sauce has thickened. The sauce may be left chunky or may be puréed with an immersion blender.

Makes 450 ml (1 pint)

dairy-free béchamel sauce

The vegan version of the classic white sauce, this can be used as the basis of a creamy vegetable sauce. It's also good in a pie filling with ingredients such as spinach or mushrooms. For a cheese-style sauce, stir in 125 g (4 oz) cheddar-style vegan 'cheese' after the sauce has thickened.

3 tbsp soya margarine
3 tbsp plain flour
375 ml (12 fl oz) soya milk

pinch ground nutmeg
sea salt and white pepper

Melt the butter in a saucepan, then stir in the flour and cook over low heat for 2 minutes, stirring constantly. Slowly add the soya milk, increase the heat slightly and bring to the boil, stirring until the sauce thickens. Add the nutmeg and season to taste with salt and pepper.
Makes 375 ml (12 fl oz)

wholemeal pastry

This is a basic wholemeal pastry. If substituting white plain flour, omit the baking powder. White vegetable fat is used here because its high fat content makes for a crispy crust, but a solid margarine may also be used, or the two can be combined. If using for a dessert, add 1 tablespoon caster sugar. Make one-and-a-half times the recipe for a 25-cm (9-inch) plate. Well wrapped, the uncooked pastry freezes well, either as a ball or rolled out on a foil plate.

225 g (8 oz) wholemeal flour
1 tsp baking powder
1 tbsp sugar (for sweet crusts only)
pinch salt

125 g (4 oz) white vegetable fat
125 g (4 oz) soya margarine
4–5 tbsp cold water

In a food processor fitted with a metal blade, pulse the flour, baking powder, sugar and salt. Add vegetable fat and margarine, pulsing until mixture resembles breadcrumbs. If making the pastry by hand, mix flour, baking powder, sugar and salt in a bowl. Using a pastry cutter, two knives or fingertips, rub in the butter until the mixture resembles coarse meal. Add 3 tablespoons of the cold water to the mixture, pulsing until clumps form, stopping to test the if dough is moist enough to hold together. If dough is too dry, add a little more water. Remove blade and draw dough into a ball. For a handmade crust, follow the same principles, stirring in the water with a knife. Wrap in clingfilm and refrigerate at least 15 to 20 minutes.
Makes one 20- to 25-cm (8- to 10-inch) tart or one small 18-cm (7-inch) pie

crisp fried tofu

Serve this fried tofu with stirfried vegetables or with the tomato sauce above.

3 tbsp nutritional yeast
3 tbsp flour
2 tsp garlic powder
$^1/_2$ tsp salt

$^1/_2$ tsp paprika
500 g (1 lb) firm or extra-firm tofu, pressed and
    cut into 1-cm ($^1/_2$-inch) pieces
2 tbsp olive oil

In a small bowl, combine the nutritional yeast, flour, garlic powder, salt and paprika. Toss in the tofu and ensure that the cubes are evenly coated. In a large frying pan, heat the olive oil over medium heat, then add the tofu. Cook, turning from time to time, until the tofu is crisp and golden brown.

Serves 4

baked marinated tofu

Given its Asian roots, a Chinese-style marinade complements the flavour and texture of tofu to perfection.

1 tbsp rice vinegar
1 tbsp sesame oil
2 tbsp soya sauce
2 tsp sugar
2 cloves of garlic, crushed
1 tbsp grated root ginger

2 spring onions, finely chopped
$^1/_2$ tsp each ground cumin & coriander
$^1/_4$ tsp dried thyme
pinch each black & cayenne peppers
500 g (1 lb) extra-firm tofu, pressed and cut
    into 1-cm ($^1/_2$-inch) thick slices

Put all the ingredients except the tofu in a bowl and combine. Put the tofu slices in a baking dish, cover with the marinade and refrigerate overnight, turning once while marinating. Preheat the oven to 190°C (375°F/Gas mark 5). Drain off excess marinade. Bake tofu for 15 minutes, turn over and bake for another 15 minutes, until tofu has developed crusty edges.

Serves 4

breakfasts & brunches

Just because you don't eat eggs and bacon doesn't mean that breakfast has to be a mean affair. Here are some delicious and nutritious treats to welcome in the new day.

breakfast parfait

see variations page 37

This breakfast not only looks delicious, but is also high in protein and keeps you full all morning.

750ml (1¼ pt) soya yoghurt
50 ml (2 fl oz) maple syrup
300g (10 oz) cooked wheat berries

225 g (8 oz) fresh strawberries, sliced
120g (4 oz) fresh blueberries
4 tsp flax seeds

Mix the yoghurt and the maple syrup together. Then, arrange the ingredients in layers in 4 large glasses. First, place one-third of the yoghurt in the base of the glass, followed by wheat berries, then top with the fruit. Sprinkle 1 teaspoon of the flax seeds over the top of each.

Serves 4

oaty apple pancakes

see variations page 38

These healthy, low-fat pancakes are a tasty way to start the day and are very quick to make. They are delicious with cranberry syrup or try them with warmed apple sauce.

50 g (2 oz) plain flour
75 g (3 oz) quick-cooking oats
2 tsp baking powder
1 tbsp brown sugar
1 tbsp vegetable oil

1 medium-tart apple, shredded
1 tsp ground cinnamon
250 ml (8 fl oz) oat milk or apple juice
1–2 tbsp sunflower oil, for frying
warmed maple syrup, to serve

Mix flour, oats, baking powder, sugar, vegetable oil, shredded apple and cinnamon together in a large mixing bowl add sufficient oat milk for form a batter. Lightly oil a non-stick frying pan or griddle with sunflower oil and place over medium heat.

Carefully pour about half a ladleful of the pancake batter into the pan. Fry until lightly browned on one side, then flip and cook the second side. Keep warm. Repeat with remaining batter. Serve with warmed maple syrup.

Makes 10–12 pancakes

scrambled tofu

see variations page 39

Tasty and nutritious on its own with thick slices of good wholemeal bread, this dish is even better accompanied by luscious fried tomatoes, fried potato and maybe vegan sausages.

1 350-g (12-oz) package firm tofu
1 tbsp vegetable oil
1 small onion, chopped
1 clove garlic, crushed

1 tsp powdered turmeric
1–2 tbsp soya sauce
lots of black pepper

Drain the tofu and crumble it with your hands into a bowl. Heat the oil in a frying pan over medium heat and gently fry the onion and garlic until softened, 4 to 5 minutes. Add the turmeric, then stir in the tofu. Reduce the heat slightly and season with soya sauce and black pepper to taste. Serve hot.

Serves 4

30   breakfasts & brunches

french toast

see variations page 40

Use your favourite bread in this recipe. Wholemeal bread is good and healthy while challah or brioche makes your French toast light and airy.

2 tbsp silken tofu
225 ml (8 fl oz) oat or soya milk
1 tbsp nutritional yeast
1 tbsp sugar
1 tsp vanilla essence
$^1/_2$ tsp ground cinnamon

pinch ground nutmeg
rapeseed oil or non-dairy margarine, for frying
8 slices bread
warmed maple syrup, to serve

In a medium bowl, blend the tofu to a paste with a little of the oat or soya milk. When smooth, add the remaining milk, nutritional yeast, sugar, vanilla, cinnamon and nutmeg.

Lightly oil a large frying pan or griddle with rapeseed oil or non-dairy margarine. Dip the bread slices into the mixture, covering both sides. Cook over medium-low heat, flipping once, until golden on both sides. Cut into triangles and serve with warmed maple syrup.

Serves 4

quick & easy breakfast bars

see variations page 41

Here's an on-the-go high-energy breakfast for those not-so-relaxed mornings. These bars are great for lunchboxes, too.

75 g (3 oz) quick-cooking rolled oats
125 g (4 oz) wholemeal flour
125 g (4 oz) brown sugar
1/4 tsp bicarbonate of soda
1/4 tsp salt
1/4 tsp ground cinnamon
pinch ground nutmeg

4 tbsp sunflower seeds
4 tbsp shredded coconut
4 tbsp dried cranberries
1 tbsp flax seeds
1 tbsp sesame seeds
125 ml (4 fl oz) rapeseed oil
3 tbsp cranberry juice

Heat oven to 170°C (325°F/Gas mark 3) and lightly oil an 20x20-cm (8x8-inch) baking tin. Combine all the dry ingredients, then stir in the oil and cranberry juice and mix well. Press the mixture into the baking pan and bake for 30 to 35 minutes until browned. Let the loaf cool for 5 minutes, then cut into slices. Will keep for 1 week in an airtight container.

Makes 12 bars

fluffy pancakes

see variations page 42

What a treat to start the day with these light and fluffy pancakes. Be sure to use white flour, because wholemeal flour makes them heavy.

225 g (8 oz) plain flour
1 heaped tbsp soya flour
2 tsp baking powder
¹/₂ tsp bicarbonate of soda
pinch salt
25 g (1 oz) caster sugar
250 ml (8 fl oz) soya milk

¹/₂ tsp vanilla essence
sunflower oil, for frying
warmed maple syrup and non-dairy butter/
    margarine, to serve

In a large bowl combine flour, soya flour, baking powder, bicarbonate of soda, salt and sugar. Add the soya milk and vanilla and stir until you have quite a thick batter.

Lightly oil a non-stick frying pan or griddle with sunflower oil and place over a medium heat. Gently pour a ladleful of batter into the pan. Wait until bubbles appear all over the surface of the pancake, then flip it over and cook on the other side until golden brown. Continue with the remaining batter while keeping the cooked pancakes warm under a clean cloth.

Stack the pancakes on small plates and serve with warmed maple syrup and non-dairy butter/margarine.

Makes 8–10 pancakes

orange marmalade bran muffins

see variations page 43

These high-fibre muffins are deceptively light and full of flavour. The mixture keeps for at least two weeks in an airtight container in the fridge, so make a double recipe and bake a fresh batch each morning.

50 g (2 oz) wheat bran
125 ml (4 fl oz) boiling water
125 ml (4 fl oz) rapeseed oil
175 g (6 oz) brown sugar
egg replacer or egg substitute for 1 egg
   (pages 23–24)

250 ml (8 fl oz) soya milk
150 g (5 oz) wholemeal flour
1¼ tsp bicarbonate of soda
½ tsp salt
300 g (10 oz) orange marmalade

Preheat the oven to 200°C (400°F/Gas mark 6). Line a muffin tin with paper muffin cases.

In a bowl, mix all the ingredients in order. Spoon into the muffin cases, filling to about the three-quarters level. Bake the muffins for 20 to 25 minutes until well risen and springy to the touch. Cool for 5 minutes, then transfer the muffins to a wire rack to finish cooling.

Makes about 10 large or 16 small muffins

variations

breakfast parfait

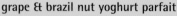

see base recipe page 27

grape & brazil nut yoghurt parfait
Prepare the basic recipe, using 175 g (6 oz) each of halved seedless red and green grapes in place of the berries and 75 g (3 oz) chopped Brazil nuts in place of the flax seeds.

granola & berry yoghurt parfait
Prepare the basic recipe, using granola in place of the whole wheat berries.

wheat berry & apricot parfait
Prepare the basic recipe, using apricot compote in place of the whole wheat berries. To make compote, halve and stone 375 g (12 oz) fresh apricots. In a pan, dissolve 50 g (2 oz) sugar in 185 ml (6 fl oz) water, add the apricots and cook over a gentle heat for 12 to 15 minutes. Remove and allow to cool before making the parfait.

wheat berry & apple parfait
Prepare the basic recipe, using 500 g (1 lb 2 oz) apple sauce flavoured with 1 teaspoon vanilla essence and 1 tablespoon ground cinnamon in place of the berries.

oaty apple pancakes

see base recipe page 28

oaty apricot pancakes
Prepare the basic recipe, using 125 g (4 oz) chopped, plump, dried apricots in place of the shredded apple and 1 teaspoon orange rind in place of the cinnamon. Orange juice may also be used in place of the apple juice.

oaty apple pancakes with sweet spices
Prepare the basic recipe, using 1 tablespoon maple syrup in place of the sugar. Also use ½ teaspoon ground cinnamon, ¼ teaspoon ground nutmeg and pinch of ground cardamom in place of the cinnamon.

blueberry & oaty banana pancakes
Prepare the basic recipe, using 1 tablespoon maple syrup in place of the sugar and 1 small mashed banana with 75 g (3 oz) blueberries in place of the apple.

high-fibre oaty apple pancakes
Prepare the basic recipe, using whole wheat or buckwheat flour in place of the plain flour. Serve with apple sauce and raisins.

scrambled tofu

see base recipe page 30

mediterranean scrambled tofu
Prepare the basic recipe, adding half a courgette, half a red pepper and half a green pepper with the onion and ½ teaspoon dried Italian herbs in place of the turmeric.

mexican scrambled tofu with frijoles
Prepare the basic recipe, adding 1 chopped green chilli with the onion and 1 peeled and chopped tomato with the turmeric. Serve with refried beans.

scrambled tofu forestière
Prepare the basic recipe, adding 75 g (3 oz) sliced mushrooms and ½ teaspoon thyme to the softened onion and frying until mushrooms have cooked.

sunshine breakfast pocket
Prepare the basic recipe. Divide it between 4 split pita bread pockets along with sliced tomato and alfalfa sprouts.

variations

french toast

see base recipe page 31

french toast with fresh berries
Prepare the basic recipe, using raspberry syrup or another fruit syrup in place of the maple syrup. Divide 225 g (8 oz) fresh berries over the French toast (a combination of raspberries, strawberries and blueberries is delicious).

banana cinnamon french toast
Prepare the basic recipe, adding 2 small mashed bananas to the batter. Serve with maple syrup and sliced banana lightly sprinkled with cinnamon.

spiced apple french toast
Prepare the basic recipe, adding 125 g (4 oz) apple sauce to the batter. Heat an additional 375 g (12 oz) apple sauce, 1/4 teaspoon ground cinnamon and 1/8 teaspoon each of ground nutmeg and cardamom in a saucepan. Serve with the French toast.

day-before french toast
Prepare the basic recipe but do not cook. Place the prepared toasts in a single layer on a platter, cover with clingfilm and refrigerate overnight. The French toast is ready to cook the next morning. (Note: This does not work with the banana variation.)

variations

quick & easy breakfast bars

see base recipe page 33

apple & walnut breakfast bars
Prepare the basic recipe, using 50 g (2 oz) dried chopped apple in place of the cranberries, 50 g (2 oz) walnuts in place of the coconut and apple juice in place of the cranberry juice.

tropical breakfast bars
Prepare the basic recipe, using 50 g (2 oz) dried mango in place of the cranberries, 4 tablespoons pumpkin seeds in place of the sunflower seeds and mango or tropical juice in place of the cranberry juice.

chocolate-coated breakfast bars
Prepare the basic recipe. Melt 125 g (4 oz) vegan plain or milk chocolate and spread over the cooled bars.

gluten-free breakfast bars
Prepare the basic recipe, using spelt flour in place of the wholemeal flour.

variations

fluffy pancakes

see base recipe page 34

spicy currant pancakes
Prepare the basic recipe, adding 75 g (3 oz) currants, 1 teaspoon ground cinnamon, ½ teaspoon ground ginger and ¼ teaspoon ground allspice to the batter.

raspberry & vanilla pancakes
Prepare the basic recipe, stirring 65 g (2¼ oz) crushed raspberries into the batter. Also use the seeds scraped from 1 vanilla pod in place of the vanilla essence. Serve garnished with whole raspberries and soya yoghurt.

fluffy pancakes with 'bacon'
Prepare the basic recipe. Serve with 8 slices of vegan-approved bacon alternative, pan-fried in a little sunflower oil and patted dry with kitchen paper.

double blueberry pancakes
Prepare the basic recipe, adding 75 g (3 oz) fresh blueberries to the batter. Serve with blueberry syrup and garnish with blueberries.

variations

orange marmalade bran muffins

see base recipe page 36

raisin maple muffins
Prepare the basic recipe, using 150 g (5 oz) raisins in place of the marmalade.
Reduce the brown sugar to 125 g (4 oz) and add 80 ml (3 fl oz) maple syrup.

figgy ginger muffins
Prepare the basic recipe, using 125 g (4 oz) chopped plump dried figs
(pre-soaked if directed to do so on the package) and 4 tablespoons chopped
crystallised ginger in place of the marmalade.

carrot muffins
Prepare the basic recipe, using 125 g (4 oz) grated carrot and ½ teaspoon
cinnamon and ½ tsp nutmeg in place of the marmalade.

peanut butter muffins
Prepare the basic recipe, using 250 g (9 oz) peanut butter in place of
the marmalade.

soups

This selection of soups has ideas for all seasons and reflects a number of different culinary traditions. Home-cooked soups are simple to prepare, highly nutritious, economical and oh, so much better than their purchased cousins.

gazpacho

see variations page 60

A quick and easy version of the chilled classic Spanish soup. If you prepare the vegetables and herbs in advance and keep them in an airtight container in the fridge, the soup can be put together in a minute, just before serving. Gazpacho looks particularly impressive served over ice cubes in a glass dish.

2 large cloves of garlic
1 large onion, roughly chopped
1 celery stick, roughly chopped
2 400-g (14-oz) tins whole or
    chopped tomatoes
4 tbsp olive oil
1 tbsp red wine vinegar

sea salt and black pepper
1 cucumber, peeled, seeded and finely chopped
1 small red pepper, seeded and finely chopped
1 tbsp chopped fresh mint
1 tbsp chopped fresh parley
lemon wedges, to serve

Turn on the food processor and, with the motor running, drop in the garlic to finely chop. Add the onion, celery, tomatoes with juice, olive oil, vinegar and salt and pepper to taste. Blend until smooth. Refrigerate.

Just before serving, chop the cucumber, pepper, mint and parsley. Stir into the tomato soup and serve with a slice of lemon on the side.

Serves 4–6

black bean soup

see variations page 61

This is a fantastic soup for a cold day when the warming flavours of the spices work their magic. Some of the soup is puréed after cooking to produce a thickly textured soup, but you can omit this step if time is short.

350 g (12 oz) black beans, soaked in cold water
    overnight or at least 5 hours (or 3 400-g
    (14-oz) tins black beans)
6 tbsp olive oil
2 medium white onions, finely chopped
3 cloves of garlic, crushed
1 carrot, chopped
1–2 fresh red chillies, chopped
2 tsp ground cumin
¼ tsp smoked paprika

2 bay leaves
1 l (1¾ pt) vegetable stock
1 400-g (14-oz) tin whole or chopped tomatoes
small bunch of fresh thyme, stalks removed or
    1 tsp dried thyme
sea salt and freshly ground pepper
1 small red onion, sliced
chopped fresh coriander
juice of 1 lime

For dried beans only, drain the beans and place them in a saucepan with plenty of water and cook over high heat. Bring to the boil and boil rapidly for 10 minutes, then reduce heat and simmer for 1¼ to 1½ hours until soft. Drain. Heat the oil in a saucepan, then add the onion and cook over medium-high heat for 5 to 7 minutes or until the onion is soft. Add the garlic, carrot, chillies, cumin, paprika and bay leaves. Continue to cook for another 2 minutes. Add the beans with the stock, tomatoes and thyme leaves. Bring to the boil, reduce the heat, cover and simmer for 20 minutes. Remove the bay leaves, then take out about half of the soup and blend with an immersion blender or in a food processor. Return the puréed soup to the pan, stir and heat through. Season to taste with salt and pepper. Serve garnished with thin slices of red onion, chopped coriander and a squeeze of lime juice.
Serves 6–8

minestrone

see variations page 62

Long cooking time is the key to this wonderful, heady minestrone. The soup matures with time, so it is best made the day before. Don't be off place by the quantity of olive oil; treat it as a flavouring.

125 ml (4 fl oz) olive oil
2 medium onions, chopped
2 carrots, chopped
2 stalks celery, sliced
125 g (4 oz) sliced French beans
3 medium courgettes, chopped
200 g (7 oz) shredded cabbage
2 l (3½ pt) vegetable stock

1 200-g (7-oz) tin chopped tomatoes
2 tbsp nutritional yeast
1 tsp dried oregano
½ tsp dried basil
sea salt and black pepper
1 400-g (14-oz) tin cannellini beans
125 g (4 oz) orzo or other tiny pasta

Heat the oil in a saucepan, then add the onions and cook, stirring frequently for 5 to 7 minutes until golden. Stir in each of the other vegetables in turn, cooking each one for 3 minutes before adding the next. Add the stock, tomatoes, yeast, oregano and basil. Season to taste with salt and pepper. Bring to the boil, then reduce the heat to very low, cover and simmer for 2 hours. If making in advance, chill.

Reheat if required. Add the beans and orzo and cook for 15 minutes before serving.

Serves 6–8

tom yum soup

see variations page 63

This fragrant vegan version of the classic Thai soup is very light but highly nutritious. The key to success lies in the balance between sweetness, spiciness and sourness, so do taste and adjust the seasoning before serving.

1 l (1¾ pt) strongly flavoured vegetable stock
2 stalks lemongrass, white part only, grated
5-cm (2-inch) piece root ginger, peeled and chopped into thin strips
1–2 fresh red chillies, seeded and chopped
6 kaffir lime leaves
juice of 1 lime
1 tsp tamarind paste
250 ml (8 fl oz) rich coconut milk

3–4 tbsp soya sauce
1–2 tsp palm or brown sugar
chilli sauce (optional)
75 g (3 oz) sliced mixed mushrooms (e.g., white, shiitake, enoki, straw or chestnut)
2 small heads bok choy, chopped
8 cherry tomatoes, halved
350-g (12-oz) package silken tofu, chopped
whole fresh coriander leaves, to garnish

Place the first seven ingredients in a large saucepan and bring to the boil. Reduce the heat, cover and simmer for 15 minutes. Strain and return liquid to the pan.

Stir in the coconut milk, then season to taste with soya sauce, sugar and chilli sauce, if using, to achieve a tangy, sweet-sour flavour to your liking. Add the mushrooms and cook for 5 minutes or until soft. Add the bok choy and tomatoes and cook for 2 minutes. Gently add the tofu and heat through. Serve garnished with coriander leaves.

Serves 6–8

corn & jalapeño chowder

see variations page 64

Served with hot crusty bread and perhaps with some mushroom pâté (page 76), this soup makes a rich, delicious, well-balanced meal.

4 large sweetcorn cobs, shucked (or 500 g
   (1 lb 2 oz) frozen sweetcorn)
2 tbsp sunflower oil
1 large onion, chopped
2 medium potatoes, chopped

1–2 jalapeño or green chillies, chopped
500 ml (16 fl oz) soya milk
1 vegan stock cube
sea salt and black pepper
chopped fresh parsley, to garnish

If using fresh sweetcorn, place the cobs in a large saucepan in boiling water and simmer for 10 to 12 minutes until tender. Cool, reserving the cooking liquid. Using a sharp knife, remove the sweetcorn kernels.

Heat the oil in a saucepan, then add the onion and cook for 5 to 7 minutes over medium-high heat until soft. Stir in the potatoes and the jalapeño or green chilli, to taste and cook for 3 minutes more. Add 400 ml (14 fl oz) of strained reserved sweetcorn cooking liquid or water, the soya milk, stock and sweetcorn. Season to taste with salt and pepper. Bring to the boil, then reduce the heat and simmer for 15 minutes or until the potatoes are tender but still retaining their shape. Serve garnished with chopped parsley.

Serves 4–6

caribbean bean & rice soup

see variations page 65

The combination of tomato and coconut gives this soup a hint of sunshine even on the coldest of days.

1 tbsp sunflower oil
1 medium onion, chopped
2 cloves of garlic, crushed
2 stalks celery, chopped
2 carrots, chopped
1 small green pepper, seeded and chopped
1 small red pepper, seeded and chopped
2 bay leaves
2 tsp paprika
750 ml (1¼ pt) tomato juice
125 ml (4 fl oz) tomato purée

2 tsp dried thyme
750 ml (1¼ pt) vegetable stock
1 400-g (14-oz) tin coconut milk
90 g (3¼ oz) long-grain rice
1 400-g (14-oz) tin red kidney beans
sea salt and black pepper
for the croutons
125 g (4 oz) day-old bread cubes
2 tbsp olive oil
2 tsp paprika
½ tsp dried thyme

Heat the oil in a large saucepan, then add the onion and cook over medium-high heat for 5 to 7 minutes until the onion is soft. Add the garlic, celery, carrots, green and red peppers, bay leaves and paprika and continue to cook for another 5 minutes. Stir in the tomatoes, tomato purée and thyme leaves, then cook for 5 minutes. Add the stock, coconut milk and rice. Bring to the boil, reduce the heat, cover and simmer for 30 minutes. Add the kidney beans and cook for another 15 minutes. Remove the bay leaves and season to taste with salt and pepper before serving garnished with croutons. To make the croutons, toss the cubes of stale bread with the olive oil, paprika and thyme. Spread in a single layer on a baking sheet and bake at 190ºC (375°F/Gas mark 5) for 4 to 5 minutes until golden brown.

Serves 2 generously

miso soup

see variations page 66

A Japanese staple, this soup has a rich taste and is quick and easy to make. And, it is so, so much better than the packaged variety. Wakame is a tender sea vegetable that expands seven times during soaking. Do not be tempted to use dashi (Japanese stock), as it probably contains dried sardines.

5-cm (2-inch) piece wakame
1 l (1¾ pt) water
1 medium onion, finely chopped
1 large carrot, finely chopped

2 tbsp miso, dissolved in 2 tbsp water
1 tbsp mirin (sweet rice wine), (optional)
1 tbsp soya sauce
chopped fresh parsley, to garnish

Soak the wakame in 250 ml (8 fl oz) water for 10 minutes; drain. Remove the central rib and cut into small pieces. In a saucepan, boil the remaining water and add the onions, carrots and wakame pieces. Reduce the heat and simmer for 5 minutes; the vegetables should be just cooked. Remove from heat and add the dissolved miso, mirin and soya sauce. Do not reboil, because this spoils the flavour of the miso. Serve garnished with parsley.

Serves 3–4

fresh tomato & basil soup

see variations page 67

A perennial favourite, the flavour of this particular version of the soup is enhanced by slowly cooking the tomatoes in garlic-infused oil.

750 g (1½ lb) large ripe tomatoes
6 tbsp olive oil
6 cloves of garlic
1 medium onion, chopped
2 bay leaves
1 small potato, chopped

1 l (1¾ pt) vegetable stock
sea salt and white pepper
2 tbsp tomato purée (optional)
2 tbsp chopped fresh basil or 2 tsp dried basil
4 tsp vegan pesto (page 74)
    or chopped fresh basil, to garnish

Peel the tomatoes by immersing in boiling water for 10 seconds, refreshing in cold water, then slipping off the skins. Slice the tomatoes into quarters and remove the seeds.

In a saucepan, heat the olive oil, then add the whole cloves of garlic. Cook the garlic until golden brown, remove from the pan and discard. Cook the onion in the flavoured oil for 5 to 7 minutes until soft. Add the tomatoes and bay leaves, reduce the heat and allow to simmer, stirring occasionally, for 15 to 20 minutes or until the oil separates into small pools and the liquid has thickened. Stir in the chopped potatoes and coat in the rich sauce, cook for 2 minutes. Add the stock, bring to the boil, then cover and simmer for 15 minutes. Taste and season with salt and pepper, then, depending on the depth of flavour and the ripeness of the tomatoes, add tomato purée, if desired. Remove the bay leaves, add the fresh or dried basil, then blend the soup in the pan with an immersion blender or transfer to a food processor. Reheat the soup to serving temperature. Serve garnished with pesto or basil.

Serves 4–6

silky lentil soup

see variations page 68

This soul-warming soup is a meal in itself, perfect for anyone feeling under the weather. As an added bonus, children love it and you can sneak all kinds of vegetables into it without their knowledge!

1 tbsp olive oil
1 onion, roughly chopped
1 green or red pepper, seeded and
    roughly chopped
1 carrot, peeled and roughly chopped
1 courgette, roughly chopped
1 clove of garlic, crushed
1 tsp ground cumin

1 tsp ground coriander
200 g (7 oz) split red lentils, washed
1 l (1¾ pt) vegetable stock
1 400-g (14-oz) tin plum tomatoes
2 tsp tomato purée
1 bay leaf
sea salt and black pepper
fresh parsley or coriander, to garnish

Heat the oil in a saucepan, then add the onion and cook over low heat for 5 to 7 minutes until soft. Stir in the pepper, carrot and courgette and cook for 3 minutes. Add the garlic, cumin and coriander, then cook, stirring constantly, for another minute. Add the remaining soup ingredients: lentils, stock, tomatoes and juice, tomato purée and bay leaf. Bring to the boil, then reduce the heat, cover and simmer for 30 minutes, until the lentils and vegetables are very soft.

Remove the bay leaf and blend the soup with an immersion blender or in a food processor. The soup will be fairly thick, so dilute with a little more stock if you prefer it thinner. Season to taste, then reheat and serve garnished with parsley or coriander.

Serves 4–6

leek & potato soup

see variations page 69

Leeks are members of the allium (onion) family and there is good evidence to indicate that you should eat one portion of this vegetable family a day. Leeks are good sources of dietary fibre, folic acid, calcium, potassium and vitamin C and are easier to digest than onions.

2 tbsp sunflower oil
3 large leeks, chopped
2 cloves of garlic, crushed
3 medium potatoes, chopped
1 l (1¾ pt) vegetable stock
1 bay leaf

sea salt and black pepper
500 ml (16 fl oz) oat or soya milk
1 tsp dried dill
120 ml (4 fl oz) soya cream
ground nutmeg, to garnish

Heat the oil in a saucepan, then add the leeks and garlic, cover and cook over low heat for 5 minutes, stirring occasionally to avoid the leeks scorching, which will produce a bitter flavour. Add the potatoes, stock and bay leaf and season to taste with salt and plenty of black pepper. Bring to the boil, reduce the heat, then cover and simmer for about 30 minutes or until the potatoes are tender.

Remove the bay leaf and blend the soup in the pan with an immersion blender or in a food processor until smooth. Add the oat or soya milk, dill and soya cream. Heat through for 5 minutes and serve garnished with nutmeg.

Serves 4–6

variations

gazpacho

see base recipe page 45

mexican gazpacho
Prepare the basic recipe, but use 2 tablespoons coriander in place of mint and parsley and add 1 finely chopped jalapeño or green chilli, ½ teaspoon cumin and ¼ teaspoon Tabasco. Serve with lime wedges instead of lemon wedges.

chunky gazpacho
Prepare the basic recipe, but omit the tomatoes from the initial blending process. Use tinned chopped tomatoes and stir them into the blended ingredients.

bloody mary gazpacho
Prepare the basic recipe, adding 50–80 ml (2–3 fl oz) vodka or to taste.

gazpacho with spicy salsa
Prepare the basic recipe. Make salsa by combining 125 g (4 oz) chopped rocket, 1 very finely chopped jalapeño or green chilli, a pinch of sea salt and 3 tablespoons olive oil. Drizzle the salsa onto the centre of the gazpacho just before serving.

variations

black bean soup

see base recipe page 46

mixed bean soup
Prepare the basic recipe, but use 1 400-g (14-oz) tin each of butter beans, pinto beans and cannelloni beans. If you want to cook beans from scratch, select a prepared bean mix that uses beans with similar cooking times.

black bean soup with chipotle
Prepare the basic recipe, using 1–3 tablespoons chopped chipotle in adobo sauce instead of fresh chillies. Chipotle is very spicy so keep tasting until you add enough for your tastes. For a more Mexican flavour, add 250 g (9 oz) fresh or frozen sweetcorn with the tomatoes.

white bean & garlic soup
Prepare the basic recipe, using cannellini beans in place of the black beans. Increase the quantity of garlic to 4 cloves and omit the carrot, chillies, cumin and tomatoes. Stir in 125 ml (4 fl oz) soya cream just before serving garnished with plenty of chopped parsley in place of coriander.

black bean & celery soup
Prepare the basic recipe, adding 4 chopped celery stalks with the carrots.

minestrone

see base recipe page 48

smooth vegetable soup
Prepare the basic recipe, omitting the pasta. Purée the soup using an immersion blender or in a food processor.

creamed vegetable soup
Prepare the basic recipe, omitting the pasta and using 1 l (1¾ pt) vegetable stock and 250 ml (8 fl oz) soya milk. Purée the cooked soup with an immersion blender or in a food processor. Stir in 125 ml (4 fl oz) soya cream and heat through just before serving.

minestrone with tofu
Prepare the basic recipe, omitting the pasta. Press 175 g (6 oz) firm tofu well, drain, then chop into 1-cm (1-inch) cubes and toss in 2 tablespoons soya sauce. Place in a baking dish and cook at 190°C (375°F/Gas mark 5) for 10 minutes, toss gently, then bake for 5 more minutes. Add cubes to the soup with the white beans.

barley minestrone
Prepare the basic recipe, omitting the pasta. Dry roast 200 g (7 oz) barley in a heavy-based pan for 3 to 4 minutes, stirring constantly. Add to the soup with the stock.

variations

tom yum soup

see base recipe page 49

tom yum soup with galangal
Prepare the basic recipe, but add a 5-cm (2-inch) piece of galangal, chopped, with the other aromatics to the stock.

tom yum soup with broccoli
Prepare the basic recipe, omitting the bok choy. Add 1 head broccoli, cut into florets, with the mushrooms.

tom yum soup with mangetout
Prepare the basic recipe, using only 1 head bok choy and adding 125 g (4 oz) fresh mangetout.

red curry tom yum soup
Prepare the basic recipe, but omit tamarind paste and chilli sauce and use only 3 kaffir lime leaves and 1 tablespoon lime juice. Flavour with 1–2 tablespoons red Thai curry paste prior to adjusting the seasonings.

variations

sweetcorn & jalapeño chowder

see base recipe page 50

roasted sweetcorn & jalapeño chowder
Prepare the basic recipe, but cook the sweetcorn cobs in water for only 5 minutes, remove and pat dry. Lightly oil the cobs with a little sunflower oil and place under a grill or on the barbeque. Cook for 3 to 5 minutes or until the kernels are just beginning to char, then continue to turn until the whole cob is roasted.

sweetcorn, kale & roast butternut squash chowder
Prepare the basic recipe, using only 2 sweetcorn cobs or 500 g (1 lb 2 oz) of frozen sweetcorn and omitting potatoes. Roast 1 small, chopped butternut squash tossed in a little oil at 180°C (350°F/Gas mark 4) for 30 minutes or until lightly caramelised, then add to the soup with the sweetcorn. Cook for 10 minutes, then add 150 g (5 oz) shredded kale and cook for 5 minutes.

sweetcorn, sweet potato & jalapeño chowder
Prepare the basic recipe, using sweet potato in place of the potato.

sweetcorn, cauliflower & jalapeño chowder
Prepare the basic recipe, using only 2 sweetcorn cobs or 250 g (8 oz) frozen sweetcorn and 1 potato. Add half a head of cauliflower, cut into half florets, with the sweetcorn.

variations

caribbean bean & rice soup

see base recipe page 53

caribbean black bean & rice soup
Prepare the basic recipe, using tinned black beans in place of the kidney beans.

curried bean & rice soup
Prepare the basic recipe, using 1–2 tablespoons medium curry paste in place of the paprika and thyme. Omit the croutons and serve with flat bread.

caribbean bean & wild rice soup
Prepare the basic recipe, using wild rice in place of the long-grain rice.

creole bean & rice recipe
Prepare the basic recipe, using smoked paprika in place of paprika and adding ½ teaspoon oregano, 1 teaspoon cumin and a pinch of cayenne pepper. Slice 225 g (8 oz) vegan sausages into the soup 15 minutes before the end of cooking. (Smoked or spicy sausage varieties would be the best choice).

variations

miso soup

see base recipe page 54

miso, ginger & spinach soup
Prepare the basic recipe, omitting the wakame. Add 2 teaspoons grated root ginger with the onion and carrots, cook for 3 minutes, then add 125 g (4 oz) chopped spinach and cook for 2 minutes until wilted. Remove from heat and finish as for the basic recipe.

miso & asparagus soup
Prepare the basic recipe, omitting wakame. Add 4 asparagus spears, finely sliced on the diagonal, at the same time as the carrot.

miso, bok choy & tofu soup
Prepare the basic recipe, omitting wakame. Cook the carrots for 2 minutes, then add 1 head shredded bok choy and cook for another 3 minutes. Add 125 g (4 oz) cubed silken tofu with the miso paste.

miso & oyster mushroom soup
Prepare the basic recipe, omitting the wakame. Add 75 g (3 oz) sliced oyster mushrooms at the same time as the carrot.

variations

fresh tomato & basil soup

see base recipe page 55

cream of tomato & basil soup
Prepare the basic recipe, replacing half the stock with 500 ml (16 fl oz) soya milk.
Serve garnished with soya cream in place of pesto or basil.

quick tomato & basil soup
Prepare the basic recipe, but use two 400-g (14-oz) tins chopped tomatoes, with
juice, instead of fresh tomatoes. Cook in the flavoured oil for 5 minutes or longer
if possible; the longer the cooking, the richer the flavour.

fresh tomato & red pepper soup
Prepare the basic recipe, omitting the basil and adding 2 seeded and sliced red
peppers and 1 teaspoon paprika with the stock. Purée as instructed or leave
chunky as desired. Serve garnished with basil in place of pesto.

fresh tomato & orange soup
Prepare the basic recipe, omitting the basil and adding the rind and juice of 2
oranges and 1 teaspoon nutmeg with the stock. Use coriander to garnish in place
of basil or pesto.

minted fresh tomato soup
Prepare the basic recipe, using chopped fresh mint in place of the basil. Add
1 tablespoon lemon juice to the finished soup. Use mint to garnish.

variations

silky lentil soup

see base recipe page 56

chunky french lentil soup
Prepare the chunky lentil soup variation above and use French lentils in place of red lentils, 2 sliced celery sticks in place of the courgette and green not red pepper. Garnish with parsley.

silken yellow pea soup
Prepare the basic recipe, using 200 g (7 oz) yellow split peas, soaked overnight in cold water, in place of red lentils. Increase the cooking time to 60 minutes.

mulligatawny soup
Prepare the basic recipe, adding 1 peeled, cored and chopped green apple with the vegetables. Use 1–2 tablespoons medium curry powder or to taste, in place of the ground cumin and add 1 teaspoon dried mint. Stir 1 tablespoon lime juice into the blended soup.

lentil soup with baby spinach
Prepare the basic recipe. Stir 225 g (8 oz) baby spinach into the soup when reheating and cook just until wilted. There is no need to garnish this variation.

leek & potato soup

see base recipe page 59

vichyssoise
Prepare the basic recipe, allow to cool, then pass through a mesh strainer to ensure the soup is absolutely smooth. Chill in the fridge before serving.

creamy potato soup
Prepare the basic recipe, replacing the leeks with 1 large yellow onion. Use soya milk in place of rice or oat milk.

creamy german potato soup
Prepare the creamy potato soup recipe above. When the onion has softened, add 1½ tablespoons celery seeds, 1 tablespoon caraway seeds and 1 tablespoon cumin seeds and cook for 1 minute. Blending this soup is optional.

creamy roast potato & garlic soup
Prepare the creamy potato soup recipe above. Preheat oven to 200°C (400°F/Gas mark 6). Place 6 unpeeled cloves of garlic in a small baking dish and drizzle with olive oil. Bake for 20 minutes, until the outside is lightly browned and cloves of garlic are soft. When cool enough to touch, squeeze each clove to extract softened garlic. Stir garlic pulp into the soup at the same time as the stock.

starters

Most cuisines have a selection of starters that are

perfect for vegans. This chapter includes recipes to

pass at parties and others that work well at formal

dinner parties. Some of these recipes also make

great light meals, served with a salad and some

good bread.

bissara

see variations page 87

This North African bean dish is very popular in Egypt where it is served with flat bread and fresh vegetable sticks. Fava beans are also known as broad beans.

350g (12 oz) large dried broad beans, soaked
   overnight and drained
3 cloves garlic
125 ml (4 fl oz) olive oil
2 l (3½ pt) water
1 small green chilli, seeded and chopped

4 tbsp lemon juice
2 tsp ground cumin
sea salt and black pepper
paprika
chopped fresh parsley, to garnish

Place the broad beans, garlic, half the olive oil and water in a saucepan. Bring to the boil, cover, then cook over medium heat until the beans are tender, about 1 to 1½ hours, depending on size and freshness of the beans. Drain and cool, reserving about 375 ml (12 fl oz) of the cooking liquid.

Place the beans and the green chilli in a food processor with 250 ml (8 fl oz) of the reserved liquor. Blend until smooth, adding more of the liquid if necessary to achieve a firm but soft purée. Return the purée to a clean saucepan and stir in the lemon juice, cumin and salt and pepper to taste. Cook gently for 5 minutes, stirring. Transfer the bissara to a serving bowl. Drizzle with the remaining olive oil, sprinkle with paprika to taste and garnish with parsley. Serve at room temperature with flat bread and vegetable sticks, if desired.

Serves 6

samosas & fresh mango chutney

see variations page 88

These delicious, spicy Indian starters are easy to make with filo pastry. Once you have mastered the first one, constructing the samosas is really easy. For tips on working with filo pastry see page 15.

4 tbsp sunflower oil
1 tsp mustard seeds
2 small onions, finely chopped
2 tsp curry powder
¼ tsp salt
2 potatoes, peeled and finely chopped
1 carrot, peeled and finely chopped
125 g (4 oz) diced French beans
125 g (4 oz) frozen peas
150 ml (5 fl oz) water

1 270-g (9½-oz) package filo pastry
sunflower oil, for deep-frying

for the chutney
1 ripe mango
1 large shallot, peeled and roughly chopped
2 green chillies, roughly chopped
2 garlic cloves
sea salt

Warm the oil in a frying pan, add the mustard seeds and cook over moderate heat until they begin to pop. Stir in the onions and fry for 5 minutes until they are soft. Add the curry powder and salt, fry for 1 minute, then add the potatoes, carrot, beans, peas and water. Cook for 15 minutes on low heat, stirring occasionally, until the vegetables are tender and the liquid almost evaporated. Remove from the heat and allow to cool. Cut the filo pastry sheets in half to make long strips. Work with one strip at a time, covering the remaining strips with wax paper or a damp cloth to prevent drying out. Place a spoonful of the filling at one end of the strip. Fold over the corner diagonally to form a triangle. Continue the folding to the end of the strip. Seal the ends with a little water. Repeat with the remaining strips.

Serves 4

Two-thirds fill a deep-fryer or wok with sunflower oil and heat to 180°C (350°F/Gas mark 4). Fry the samosas two at a time for 2 to 3 minutes until golden. Drain on paper towel, then serve hot or at room temperature.

To make the chutney, peel the mango and slice the flesh from the stone, roughly chop and set aside. In a food processor, process the shallot, chillies and garlic until smooth. Add the mango and pulse to roughly chop. Season with salt. Transfer to a serving bowl.

spaghettini with pesto

see variations page 89

Pesto comes from Genoa in northern Italy and is made from basil, olive oil, pine kernels along with Parmesan or Pecorino cheese. This vegan version uses nutritional yeast in place of the cheese and tastes just as good. Leftover pesto can be stored in the fridge for a few days. Simply spoon it into a jar and cover it with a thin layer of olive oil. It is great on potatoes, runner beans or stirred into tomato sauce or soup.

40 g (1½ oz) pine kernels
50 g (2 oz) fresh basil leaves, washed and
    patted dry
3 cloves garlic
4 tbsp nutritional yeast

1 tsp lemon juice
185 ml (6 fl oz) olive oil
sea salt and black pepper
350 g (12 oz) spaghettini
small black olives (optional)

First, make the pesto. Place the pine kernels in a frying pan over a moderate heat and toast until golden brown, turning continuously to prevent burning. Allow to cool; put the basil, pine kernels, garlic and nutritional yeast in a blender, turn on and gradually add the olive oil in a thin stream until the pesto is the desired consistency. Season to taste with salt and pepper.

Cook the spaghettini in a saucepan of boiling water for approximately 5 minutes or as stated on the package. Drain and toss with the pesto and garnish with black olives, if desired. Serve immediately.

Serves 4

spinach vadai & coconut chutney

see variations page 90

In India no railway journey would be complete without the smell of freshly cooked vadai at every station. Vadai make great starters and are perfect for lunch boxes.

200 g (7 oz) yellow split peas (chana dal)
125 g (4 oz) shredded fresh spinach, washed
1 small onion, finely chopped
1–1½ green chillies, finely chopped
1 tsp grated root ginger
5 curry leaves, finely chopped
½ tsp garam masala or turmeric
2 tbsp chopped fresh coriander
sea salt
sunflower oil, to fry

for the coconut chutney
125 g (4 oz) freshly grated coconut
2 tbsp chopped onion
1 fresh green chilli
2 tbsp chopped fresh coriander
1 tbsp lemon or lime juice
sea salt
1 tbsp black mustard seeds

Soak the split peas for at least 2 hours and then drain. Meanwhile, cook the washed spinach until wilted in a saucepan with no water other than that clinging to the leaves; drain and cool. To make the chutney, combine all the ingredients except the mustard seeds in a blender until coarsely ground, adding a little water if necessary. Heat the mustard seeds in a hot dry pan until they pop. Add to the chutney and adjust the seasoning to taste. Set aside until ready to serve. Place the drained peas in a food processor and blend to a coarse paste without adding any water. Tip into a bowl and stir in the cooked spinach and the remaining ingredients. Using wet hands form the mixture into small round patties about 4 cm (1¼ inch) in diameter. Heat a little sunflower oil in a frying pan and fry the vadai in batches, turning to ensure that they are golden brown all over. Drain on kitchen paper and keep warm until serving, with the chutney.
Serves 4

mushroom herb pâté

see variations page 91

Whether you serve this tasty pâté as an elegant starter or as a sandwich filling,
you'll enjoy the pungent, earthiness of the mushrooms. Portabella mushrooms are
used here for their strong flavour, but there are many mushrooms to choose from.
Just pick your favourite.

2 tbsp olive oil
1 medium onion, chopped
2 cloves of garlic, crushed
500 g (1 lb 2 oz) Portabella mushrooms, sliced
1 sprig fresh rosemary
125 g (4 oz) sunflower seeds

rind of 1 lemon
2 tbsp nutritional yeast
pinch ground nutmeg
1 tbsp chopped fresh parsley
1 tbsp chopped fresh thyme
sea salt and black pepper

Heat the oil in a large saucepan, then add the onion and cook over medium–high heat for 5
to 7 minutes until the onion is soft. Add the garlic, mushrooms and rosemary and cook until
the mushrooms are tender. Continue to cook until most of the liquid has evaporated; cool.
Remove the rosemary.

Place the mushroom mixture in a food processor along with the remaining ingredients.
Process until smooth, scraping down the sides once in a while. Shape the pâté into oval
quenelles: heat a dessert spoon in hot water, then, leaving it wet, scoop up some pâté and
roll it between the bowl and the spoon to form a quenelle. Slide it off the spoon and onto a
plate. Alternatively, press into ramekin dishes and garnish with fresh herbs. Serve at room
temperature with crackers or toast.

Serves 4

melon with ginger & orange syrup

see variations page 92

Ginger is said to be good for the digestion, which makes it the perfect ingredient to enjoy at the start of a meal. The syrup may be made a day or two ahead of time.

for the syrup
4 tbsp water
4 tbsp fresh orange juice
2 tbsp chopped and peeled gingerroot
3–4 strips orange rind
1–2 tbsp agave syrup

for the melon
1 ripe cantaloupe or honeydew melon
4 tbsp finely chopped crystallised ginger
fresh mint, to garnish

To make the syrup, combine the water orange juice, ginger and orange rind in a saucepan, then sweeten to taste with agave nectar. Bring to the boil, then reduce the heat and simmer for 2 minutes. Remove from the heat and allow to stand 15 minutes, then remove and discard the ginger and orange rind while the syrup is still warm. Cool, then chill for at least 1 hour or longer if desired.

Arrange the melon on plates in slices or make melon balls and place in bowls. Sprinkle the stem ginger on top; chill. Just before serving, drizzle with the syrup and garnish with fresh mint.

Serves 4

cashew spread

see variations page 93

This is the vegan version of a cheese spread. Serve it as a starter with vegetable crudités, breadsticks or crackers, but it is also a great sandwich filler and it works well on baked potatoes. Using raw cashews creates a delicately flavoured spread, while toasted cashews produce a fuller flavour.

175 g (6 oz) raw or roasted unsalted cashews
water, to soak
juice of ½ lemon
4 tbsp water
1 large clove of garlic
2 tbsp nutritional yeast
1 tsp balsamic condiment
½ tsp sugar

½ tsp sea salt or to taste
½ tsp white pepper or to taste
2 tbsp toasted sesame seeds
1 tbsp chopped spring onion
1 tbsp chopped fresh parsley
2 tsp chopped fresh thyme
fresh herbs and a slice of lemon, to garnish

Soak the cashews for at least an hour in water; drain. Combine the cashews, lemon juice, water, garlic, nutritional yeast, balsamic condiment and sugar in a food processor. Process until smooth, scraping down the sides once in a while. Season to taste with salt and white pepper.

Transfer the mixture to a bowl. Stir in the sesame seeds, spring onion and herbs. Serve at room temperature garnished with fresh herbs and lemon.

Serves 4–6

tomato bruschetta

see variations page 94

Here bruschetta is made from big slices of crispy ciabatta, but if you make bruschetta from sliced baguette it becomes perfect finger food. Serve with drinks, especially because it is just as good eaten hot or cold.

4 large, thick slices ciabatta
1 garlic clove, halved
2 tbsp extra-virgin olive oil
sea salt and black pepper

3 fresh tomatoes, skinned, seeded and chopped
8 sun-dried tomatoes in oil, roughly chopped
15 g ($\frac{1}{2}$ oz) torn fresh basil leaves
oil from jar of sun-dried tomatoes

Preheat the oven to 190°C (375°F/Gas mark 4). Rub each slice of ciabatta with the cut sides of the clove of garlic. Arrange the bread on a baking tray and drizzle with the olive oil. Season with salt and bake for about 10 minutes, turning once, until golden.

Mix the tomatoes, sun-dried tomatoes and half the basil together. Season to taste with salt and pepper. Spoon on top of the ciabatta slices, then drizzle with a little of the oil from the sun-dried tomatoes. Return to the oven for 3 minutes to heat through. Serve garnished with the rest of the basil.

Serves 4

spiced chickpeas

see variations page 95

These tasty little chickpeas are great served with drinks or sprinkled over a salad for added protein. Be warned, they are addictive! They are best eaten the day they are made.

1½ tsp ground cumin
1 tsp cayenne pepper
1 tsp smoked paprika
½ tsp sugar

2 tbsp olive oil
1 400-g (14-oz) tin chickpeas, drained
1–2 tbsp tamari

Combine the cumin, cayenne, paprika and sugar in a bowl and set aside. Place the oil in a frying pan over medium heat and cook the chickpeas for about 10 minutes until they are golden brown. Add the spice mixture and toss to combine. Drizzle with the tamari, stirring until evenly coated. Transfer to a plate and cool to room temperature, tossing occasionally to separate.

Serves 4

tapenade with crudités

see variations page 96

This classic dish is usually flavoured with anchovies, so if you are tempted to buy your tapenade, check the ingredients carefully. The vegetables sticks can be prepared a few hours in advance and kept in an airtight container in the fridge until needed.

for the tapenade
20 black olives, pitted
2 tbsp capers
rind and juice of 1 lemon
5 garlic cloves, crushed
180 ml (6 fl oz) olive oil
sea salt and black pepper

lemon slices, to garnish
for the vegetable sticks
1 red pepper
8 celery stalks
8 baby carrots
½ cucumber
8 radishes

To make the tapenade, place the olives, capers, lemon juice and rind, garlic and oil in a food processor and blend until smooth. Season to taste with salt and pepper, being careful with the salt because the olives and capers are both already high in salt. Transfer to a serving bowl and garnish with lemon slices.

Cut the pepper into strips. Scrub the carrots with a brush under cold running water to clean, if necessary, cut in half lengthwise. Wash the celery and cut into strips. Cut the cucumber into sticks. Wash and trim the radishes. Arrange decoratively on a plate and serve with the tapenade.

Serves 4

hummus with dukkah

see variations page 97

Making your own hummus is a great money saver and you get to select organic ingredients and adjust the acidity, spices and texture to suit your tastebuds. You may not need all the dukkah, but keep it in a sealed container and use it on salads or vegetable dishes. Serve this hummus as a dip with toasted pita bread.

for the hummus
1 small onion, chopped
2 tsp olive oil
4 garlic cloves, minced
1 400-g (14-oz) tin chickpeas (or equivalent in
    home-cooked beans)
125 g (4 oz) tahini
4 tbsp lemon juice
4 tbsp fresh chopped parsley
2 tbsp chopped jalapeño peppers (optional)

1 tsp cumin
1/4 tsp cayenne pepper
1 tsp salt
for the dukkah
40 g (1 1/2 oz) sesame seeds
40 g (1 1/2 oz) flaked almonds
2 tbsp coriander seeds
1 tsp cumin seeds
sea salt and black pepper

To make the hummus, heat the olive oil in a saucepan and cook the onions for 5 to 7 minutes, until soft. Place the onions and all the other ingredients in a food processor and blend until the hummus reaches your desired texture, adding a little water, if the mixture appears too stiff. To make the dukkah, combine the seeds and almonds in a hot, dry frying pan. Toast until golden, then cool. Coarsely grind mixture by pulsing a couple of times in a food processor or by lightly crushing with a pestle and mortar. Season to taste with the salt and pepper. Sprinkle dukkah over the top of the hummus to serve.

Serves 4–6

variations

bissara

see base recipe page 71

bissara with grilled courgette
Prepare the basic recipe and spread it onto a platter. Slice 2 courgette lengthwise and lay on a baking tray. Sprinkle with lemon juice and a little salt and pepper. Put under a hot grill until just beginning to char round the edges. Alternatively, cook the courgette on a grill. Place the courgette slices over the bissara.

pinto bean purée
Prepare the basic recipe, using pinto beans in place of broad beans.

white bean & garlic purée
Prepare the basic recipe, using haricot beans in place of broad beans and adding 1 or 2 more garlic cloves.

fresh broad bean bissara
Prepare the basic recipe, using 1 kg (2¼ lb) fresh broad beans in place of the dried broad beans. To cook, remove the beans from their pods and cook in boiling water for 10 minutes, until tender; drain and refresh with cold water. Remove the skins from the beans to reveal the bright green beans inside. Continue as for basic recipe.

variations

samosas & fresh mango chutney

see base recipe page 72

samosas & minted yoghurt
Prepare the basic samosas. In place of the chutney, serve with 250ml (8 fl oz) Greek-style yoghurt mixed with 4 tablespoons chopped fresh mint and 2 teaspoons lime juice. Serve garnished with paprika and fresh mint leaves.

potato, spinach & cashew samosas with fresh mango chutney
Prepare the basic samosas, omitting carrots, beans and peas. After the potatoes are tender, add 125 g (4 oz) broken cashews and cook for 2 minutes, then add 125 g (4 oz) chopped fresh spinach and cook until wilted. Stir in 4 tablespoons chopped fresh coriander. Allow to cool, then proceed with recipe.

sweet potato & ginger samosas with fresh mango chutney
Prepare the basic samosas, using chopped sweet potatoes in place of the potato and omitting the carrots and beans. Add 2 teaspoons grated root ginger and 1 finely chopped green chilli with the curry powder.

oven-baked samosas with fresh mango chutney
Prepare the basic recipe, but instead of deep-frying, brush samosas with sunflower oil and place on a parchment-lined baking tray. Bake at 200°C (400°F/ Gas mark 6) for 10 to 12 minutes.

variations

spaghettini with pesto

see base recipe page 74

rocket pesto
Prepare the basic pesto recipe, replacing the pine nuts with walnuts and the basil leaves with rocket leaves.

coriander pesto
Prepare the basic pesto recipe, replacing the basil leaves with coriander leaves.

watercress pesto
Prepare the basic pesto recipe, replacing the pine nuts with walnuts and the basil leaves with watercress leaves.

sun-dried tomato pesto
Prepare the basic recipe, then stir in 65 g (2¼ oz) sun-dried tomatoes (in oil), drained and chopped.

spinach vadai & coconut chutney

see base recipe page 75

plain vadai in yoghurt sauce
Prepare basic vadai, omitting the spinach. In place of the chutney, make a sauce with 500 ml (16 fl oz) soya yoghurt, 2 tablespoons water and ¼ teaspoon each of salt and sugar, or to taste. Pour over vadai and garnish with red chilli powder, ground cumin and fresh coriander leaves.

vadai & fresh tomato chutney
Prepare basic vadai. Make a tomato chutney by combining 3 skinned and chopped tomatoes with 1 finely chopped red onion, 25 g (1 oz) freshly chopped mint, 1 tablespoon chilli-flavoured oil and 1 teaspoon toasted cumin seeds.

vadai & fresh mango chutney
Prepare basic vadai. Serve with mango chutney (page 72).

red chilli vadai & coconut chutney
Prepare the basic recipe, but make a hotter version by using red chillies in place of the green chillies.

mushroom herb pâté

see base recipe page 76

mexican pâté
Prepare the basic recipe, but add 1 to 2 chopped red chilli peppers with the mushrooms and use 4 tablespoons chopped fresh coriander in place of the rosemary, parsley and thyme. Serve with chunks of avocado dipped in lime juice.

mushroom, herb & walnut pâté
Prepare the basic recipe, but replace the sunflower seeds with 75 g (3 oz) chopped walnuts, which have been soaked in hot water for 2 hours.

mushroom, herb & fennel pâté
Prepare the basic recipe. Toast 2 teaspoons fennel seeds in a dry frying pan for a minute or two until they start to pop. Add to the pâté after blending.

mushroom, herb & aubergine pâté
Prepare the basic recipe, using 225 g (8 oz) mushrooms and 1 small aubergine. Cut the aubergine into 1-cm (½-inch) thick slices. Sprinkle with salt and let sit for 1 hour, then wipe off the excess water with paper towels. Roughly chop and cook with the mushrooms.

variations

melon with ginger & orange syrup

see base recipe page 79

gingered melon & strawberry salad with ginger syrup
Prepare the basic syrup, using 125 ml (4 fl oz) water and omitting the orange juice and rind. Serve the melon along with 225 g (8 oz) fresh, hulled strawberries.

melon & black grape salad with gingered port syrup
Prepare the basic syrup, using 125 ml (4 fl oz) port in place of the orange juice and omitting the rind. Serve the melon along with 225 g (8 oz) black seedless grapes.

gingered melon salad
Prepare the basic recipe, using a quarter each of a cantaloupe and a honeydew melon. Add 125 g (4 oz) each of green and black seedless grapes and 2 large, sliced plums.

gingered melon & orange soup
Prepare the basic recipe. Blend the melon and the syrup in a food processor until smooth. Serve in bowls garnished with fresh mint.

variations

cashew spread

see base recipe page 80

cashew coconut spread
Prepare the basic recipe, using full-fat coconut milk in place of water. Add the herbs, if desired.

almond spread
Prepare the basic recipe, using almonds or smoked almonds in place of the cashews and 3 tablespoons olive oil in place of the water. Add the herbs and sesame seeds, if desired.

peppered cashew spread
Prepare the basic recipe, but omit the herbs and sesame seeds. Add 1 small 65-g (2¼-oz) jar pimentos and 1 tablespoon smoked paprika to the food processor with the cashews. For additional bite, add 1 to 2 tablespoons finely chopped chipotle in adobo sauce.

carrot & raisin cashew spread
Prepare the basic recipe, using 75 g (3 oz) grated carrot and 75 g (3 oz) raisins in place of the spring onion, parsley and thyme.

tomato bruschetta

see base recipe page 81

aubergine bruscetta
One hour before preparing, cut 1 aubergine into thick slices, sprinkle with salt and set aside. Wipe dry with kitchen paper, brush with olive oil and season with salt and pepper. Place under the grill and cook until golden on each side. Meanwhile, prepare the basic bruschetta, but omit the sun-dried tomatoes. Arrange the aubergine on top of the tomato-basil mixture. Grill and finish as in the basic recipe.

tapenade brushetta
Prepare the ciabatta, but omit the tomato topping. Spread with tapenade (page 85) and garnish each piece with ¼ cherry tomato.

portobello mushroom bruschetta
Prepare the ciabatta, but omit the tomato topping. Cook 1 onion in oil until soft, add 175 g (6 oz) sliced mushrooms and 1 teaspoon dried thyme, season with salt and pepper and cook until the mushrooms are tender. Spread on the ciabatta.

artichoke tomato bruschetta
Prepare the ciabatta. Use 1 200-g (7-oz) jar artichoke hearts, drained and chopped, on top of the tomatoes.

variations

spiced chickpeas

see base recipe page 82

spiced pecans
Prepare the basic recipe, using pecans in place of the chickpeas. Omit oil and dry roast until golden.

spiced almonds
Prepare the basic recipe, using almonds in place of the chickpeas. Omit oil and dry roast until golden.

spiced pumpkin seeds
Prepare the basic recipe, using pumpkin seeds in place of the chickpeas. Omit oil and dry roast until golden.

spiced seed mix
Prepare the basic recipe, replacing the chickpeas with 50 g (2 oz) each of pumpkin seeds, sunflower seeds and pine kernels, and 2 tablespoons each of sesame seeds and flax seeds. Omit the oil and dry roast the pumpkin seeds, sunflower seeds and pine kernels for 2 minutes. Then add the sesame seeds and flax seeds and continue to roast until golden before adding the spice mixture and tamari.

variations

tapenade with crudités

see base recipe page 85

mushroom tapenade with crudités
Prepare the basic recipe, using 200 g (7 oz) sliced mushrooms, cooked in 2 tablespoons olive oil. Do not add any more oil to the tapenade.

sun-dried tomato tapenade with crudités
Prepare the basic recipe, using rehydrated sun-dried tomatoes or drained sun-dried tomatoes in oil in place of the olives. Reduce the oil to 4 tablespoons and flavour with 2 tablespoons chopped fresh basil.

green olive tapenade with crudités
Prepare the basic recipe, using green olives in place of the black olives.

tapenade-stuffed piquillo peppers
Prepare the basic tapenade, then use it to stuff 200 g (7 oz) jarred piquillo peppers, drained. Omit the vegetable sticks.

hummus with dukkah

see base recipe page 86

black bean hummus with dukkah
Prepare the basic recipe, using black beans in place of chickpeas and coriander in place of the parsley.

pimento hummus with harissa
Prepare the basic recipe, adding 1 chopped roasted pimento (from a jar or freshly cooked). Serve with a small dish of harissa (hot chilli sauce from North Africa) in place of the dukkah.

tomato hummus pasta sauce
Prepare the basic recipe. Stir 225 g (8 oz) hummus into 1 400-g (14-oz) tin chopped tomatoes and heat through without boiling. Serve over penne, garnished, if desired, with dukkah.

hummus pitta sandwich with shredded vegetables
Prepare the basic recipe and use the hummus to stuff 4 halved pita breads along with shredded iceberg lettuce, carrot, very finely cut green pepper and alfalfa sprouts. Omit the dukkah.

salads

Preparing salads gives the vegan cook an opportunity to show flair and imagination. The availability of a dazzling array of fresh vegetables, grains and beans provides so much scope to produce really tantalising salads to tempt the eye and the palate.

green salad & ranch-style dressing

see variations page 114

A simple green salad is the perfect accompaniment to most main dishes. This vegan version of the classic American dressing has a wonderful, creamy, tangy bite that shows off the texture and flavours of the salad perfectly. The dressing may be made in advance, as it keeps for up to a week in the fridge.

for the ranch dressing
125 g (4 oz) silken tofu
4 tbsp cider vinegar
2 cloves of garlic, crushed
2 tbsp olive oil
1 tsp Dijon mustard
1 tsp maple syrup
2 tbsp chopped fresh flat-leaf parsley
1/2 tbsp fresh oregano
1/4 tbsp fresh thyme

sea salt and white pepper
oat milk, if required
for the salad
1 head cos or webb lettuce, torn into bite-size
    pieces
1 small head radicchio, torn into bite-size
    pieces
1 bunch rocket, tough stems removed
4 spring onions, thinly sliced
50 g (2 oz) alfalfa sprouts

To make the dressing, place all the ingredients except the salt, pepper and oat milk in a blender. Process until blended. Taste, season with salt and pepper and add a little oat milk to thin, if needed. Cover and refrigerate.

To make the salad, wash, dry and prepare the vegetables and place in a serving bowl.

Just before serving, pour in enough dressing to lightly coat the salad, toss gently, then serve with additional dressing on the side.

Serves 6

tabbouleh

see variations page 115

This is the national dish of Lebanon and each family has its own way of preparing it. This version is heady with the flavour of fresh herbs, but feel free to improvise and stamp your own mark on this flexible dish.

175 g (6 oz) bulgur wheat
4 tbsp lemon juice
4 tbsp virgin olive oil
1 tbsp finely chopped onion
6 spring onions, finely chopped
75 g (3 oz) flat-leaf parsley, chopped

25 g (1 oz) fresh mint, chopped
sea salt and black pepper
1 head cos lettuce
4 ripe tomatoes, quartered
fresh parsley sprigs, to garnish

Place the bulgur wheat in a bowl, cover with 500 ml (16 fl oz) boiling water and allow to stand for 20 minutes. Drain, then squeeze to remove water and transfer into a bowl. Add the lemon juice, oil, onion, spring onions, parsley and mint. Season to taste with salt and pepper. Toss, then chill for at least 1 hour.

To serve, arrange the lettuce leaves around the edge of a platter, spoon the salad in the centre and garnish with the tomatoes and sprigs of parsley.

Serves 4–6

gado gado

see variations page 116

This is an easy version of the Indonesian salad that is characterised by the spicy peanut dressing. For added protein, sliced tempeh can be added.

for the salad
2 medium potatoes
2 carrots, cut into matchsticks
125 g (4 oz) French beans, sliced
½ Chinese cabbage coarsely shredded
125 g (4 oz) bean sprouts
1 head bok choy, horizontally sliced
½ cucumber in matchstick slices
225 g (8 oz) firm tofu, drained and sliced

for the peanut dressing
250 g (9 oz) crunchy peanut butter
500 ml (16 fl oz) water
1 small onion, very finely chopped
2 cloves of garlic, crushed
1 tbsp brown sugar
1 tsp rice vinegar
½–1 tsp chilli powder
sea salt

Boil the potatoes until just tender, then cut into slices. Parboil the carrots and French beans until tender but still crisp. Blanch the bean sprouts for 10 seconds, drain; repeat with the Chinese cabbage. Layer the vegetables, the bok choy and cucumber on individual plates.

In a non-stick frying pan, fry the tofu on both sides until golden brown, then drain on kitchen paper. Cool and arrange on top of the vegetables.

To make the dressing, combine the peanut butter and water until they are well mixed. Stir in the onion, garlic, brown sugar and rice vinegar, then add chilli powder and salt to taste. Pour the dressing over the vegetables just before serving.

Serves 4

whole wheat grain salad

see variations page 117

The chewy texture of the whole wheat kernels contrasts beautifully with the soft texture of the fried onions and peppers to make a memorable salad. Serve warm or cold.

200 g (7 oz) whole wheat grain
$\frac{1}{2}$ tsp salt
3 tbsp olive oil
1 large onion, sliced
1 small red pepper, sliced
1 small green pepper, sliced

1 small yellow pepper, sliced
3 tbsp tamari soya sauce
2 tbsp chopped fresh flat-leaf parsley
black pepper
fresh parsley sprigs, to garnish

Rinse the whole wheat grains under cold water, then place them in a saucepan with the salt and plenty of water. Bring to the boil, then simmer for 60 minutes or until tender. Drain and set aside.

Meanwhile, heat the olive oil in a large frying pan and cook the onion for about 8 minutes, until golden. Add the sliced peppers and continue to cook until they are soft. Toss the onions and peppers into the whole wheat grains with the tamari, chopped parsley and plenty of black pepper. Serve garnished with parsley sprigs.

Serves 6

avocado & tomato salad

see variations page 118

The only fruit that contains more monosaturated fatty acids than the avocado is the olive. Avocados are also extremely high in potassium and are a significant source of vitamins, among which are the B-complex group, especially folic acid, which are important to those on a meat-free diet. They are also slow-burning and easy to digest. Oh yes, they are also delicious!

2 tbsp pine nuts
2 avocados, peeled, pitted and sliced
1 tbsp lemon juice
3 ripe beefsteak tomatoes, roughly chopped
1 small red onion, finely sliced
8 radishes, trimmed and sliced
2 tbsp chopped fresh basil

sea salt and black pepper
1 head cos lettuce, trimmed and roughly torn
for the dressing
3 tbsp olive oil
1 tbsp balsamic vinegar
1 small garlic clove, minced

Toast the pine kernels in a dry hot frying pan until golden, set aside and cool. Toss the sliced avocado in lemon juice to prevent browning, then combine with the tomatoes, onions and radishes. Season with salt and pepper.

Mix all the ingredients together for the dressing. Pour the dressing over the avocado-tomato mixture. Set aside for at least 30 minutes for the flavours to blend.

Line a salad bowl with the cos lettuce, gently add the avocado-tomato mixture and serve garnished with the pine kernels.

Serves 4

warm potato salad

see variations page 119

Vegans can enjoy a creamy potato salad using either a purchased dairy-free mayonnaise or by making it from scratch. The mayonnaise for this recipe is also delicious in a baked potato, on a sandwich or with your favourite salad ingredients.

for the mayonnaise
125 ml (4 fl oz) soya milk
4 tbsp lemon juice
1/2 tsp Dijon mustard
pinch paprika
approximately 185 ml (6 fl oz) mixed olive oil
    and rapeseed oil
sea salt

for the salad
750 g (1 1/2 lb) small red-skinned potatoes, diced
1 small red onion, finely chopped
1 tbsp chopped fresh dill
1 tbsp snipped fresh chives
sea salt and black pepper

To make the mayonnaise, place the soya milk, lemon juice, Dijon mustard and paprika in a bowl. Whisk to combine or use an immersion blender. Slowly add the oil in a thin stream, whisking constantly, until the mayonnaise is thick, then continue with the mixing for 1 minute longer. Chill.

Cook the potatoes in a pan of boiling salted water for 12 to15 minutes until just tender. Drain the potatoes and tip into a large bowl. Set aside until just warm. Drizzle the mayonnaise over the potatoes and gently mix. Allow to stand for at least 15 minutes to allow the potatoes to absorb the flavours. Stir the dill, chives and red onion into the potatoes, then season to taste with salt and pepper. Serve immediately.

Serves 6

spinach salad

see variations page 120

The contrasting textures and colours of the spinach, chickpeas and tomatoes make this salad look and taste like a feast, while the walnut dressing adds an interesting taste note. It is amazingly good for you too!

25 g (1 oz) pine kernels
125 g (4 oz) baby spinach, washed and dried
40 g (1½ oz) sun-dried tomatoes in extra-virgin olive oil, chopped
1 small red onion, very thinly sliced
1 avocado, peeled, stoned and sliced
1 400-g (14-oz) tin chickpeas
16 cherry tomatoes, halved

75 g (3 oz) whole, stoned black olives
for the walnut vinaigrette
2 tbsp freshly squeezed lemon juice
¼ tsp sugar
½ tsp Dijon mustard
sea salt and black pepper
4 tbsp walnut oil

Toast the pine kernels in a dry hot frying pan until golden, set aside and cool.

Place the spinach in a salad bowl. Carefully toss in the remaining salad ingredients.

To make the vinaigrette, whisk together the lemon juice, sugar, mustard and salt and pepper to taste in a medium bowl. Continue to whisk while slowly adding the walnut oil in a thin stream, to thicken. Pour the dressing over the salad and toss gently, taking care not to break up the chickpeas and avocado.

Serves 6

lentil & rice-stuffed tomatoes

see variations page 121

Conveniently, brown rice and lentils take the same time to cook, so if you substitute any other rice, cook it separately. If possible, stuff these tomatoes several hours in advance or even the day before, to allow the flavours time to blend.

125 g (4 oz) green lentils, soaked for
   at least 2 hours
125 g (4 oz) brown rice, washed
750 ml (1¹/₃ pt) vegetable stock
8 medium-large ripe tomatoes
1 jalapeño or green chilli, diced
¹/₂ cucumber, diced
75 g (3 oz) cooked sweetcorn

3 spring onions, sliced
6 tbsp chopped fresh coriander or parsley
for the dressing
4 tbsp olive oil
1 tsp grated lime rind
3 tbsp fresh lime juice
sea salt and black pepper
1 clove garlic, crushed

Drain the soaked lentils and place them in a large saucepan with the brown rice and stock. Bring to the boil, reduce the heat, cover and simmer for 35 to 45 minutes, until the rice and lentils are cooked. Drain and cool. Meanwhile, cut the tops off the tomatoes. Carefully scoop out the pulp, discarding the seeds but reserving the flesh for stuffing the tomatoes. Invert tomato shells on kitchen paper to drain. Then make the dressing by whisking together the oil, lime rind and juice, salt, pepper and garlic.

Gently stir the chilli, cucumber, sweetcorn, spring onions and coriander or parsley into the cold lentil and rice mixture along with the reserved tomato pulp and the dressing. Scoop the filling into the empty tomato cavities, packing them gently and firmly. Replace the tomato tops. Keep chilled, if making in advance, but serve at room temperature.

Serves 4 or 8

pear & endive salad with caramelised cashews

see variations page 122

Belgian endive has a bright, tangy flavour, which is balanced by the sweetness of the pear and the crispy, caramelised cashews in this salad. If you purchase the endive in advance, store in the fridge wrapped in paper, then in a plastic bag because it will turn green and bitter if exposed to light.

for the cashews
75 g (3 oz) cashews
2 tsp vegetable oil
sea salt
4 tbsp maple or agave syrup

for the salad
4 heads Belgian endive
2 ripe pears, unpeeled

for the dressing
2 tbsp white wine vinegar
1 tsp Dijon mustard
4 tbsp olive oil
salt, to taste

Line a plate with parchment paper. Preheat a heavy-bottomed saucepan over low-medium heat, then toast the cashews for about 5 minutes, tossing them frequently. Sprinkle the vegetable oil and a little salt over the cashews and toss to coat. Add the maple or agave nectar, continue to toss for about 30 seconds, until the syrup begins to bubble. Transfer to the parchment paper and allow to cool completely. Break apart. Separate some large leaves of endive and arrange them around each individual serving plate in a star pattern. Chop the remaining endive and place in the centre of the dish. Just before serving, combine all the dressing ingredients in a small bowl. Chop the pears and toss with a little of the salad dressing to prevent the pears from browning, then arrange them over the endive leaves. Sprinkle caramelised cashews over each serving.

Serves 4

spring rain salad

see variations page 123

Harusame noodles or cellophane noodles are commonly used to make delicate salads in Japan. Here they are enlivened with a spicy wasabi and pickled ginger dressing. To give this dish an authentic feel, slice the vegetables as finely as possible.

for the dressing
1 tbsp white miso
1 tbsp hot water
1 shallot, minced
1 tbsp minced pickled ginger
pinch wasabi, to taste
1 tbsp rice vinegar
1 tbsp soya sauce
125 ml (4 fl oz) grapeseed oil or canola oil

for the salad
40 g (1½ oz) dried harusame noodles or
  cellophane noodles (bean thread noodles)
1 small cucumber, cut into very thin strips
½ carrot, cut into very thin strips
1 spring onion, finely shredded

To make the dressing, mix the miso to a paste with the hot water and whisk together with the shallot, ginger, wasabi, rice vinegar and soya sauce. Slowly whisk in the oil in a thin stream, to thicken. Taste and adjust the seasoning and add more wasabi, if desired.

Bring a saucepan of water to the boil and cook the noodles according to the package directions. Refresh in cold water and drain. Mix the noodles, cucumber, carrot and spring onion in a large salad bowl or in individual serving dishes.

Just before serving, pour the dressing over the salad and toss to mix.

Serves 6

variations

green salad with ranch-style dressing

see base recipe page 99

green salad with grainy mustard dressing
Prepare the dressing, using 1 tablespoon grainy mustard in place of the
Dijon. Prepare the salad, adding half a cucumber, sliced; half a red pepper,
sliced; half a yellow pepper, sliced; 2 tomatoes, sliced; and 75 g (3 oz) small
stoned olives.

green salad with marinated tofu & ranch-style dressing
Prepare the basic recipe, adding 225 g (8 oz) prepared marinated or
herbed tofu.

green salad with chickpeas & ranch-style dressing
Prepare the basic recipe, adding 1 400-g (14-oz) tin chickpeas.

green salad with hazelnut dressing
Prepare the salad, but use hazelnut dressing in place of ranch dressing. To
make the dressing, whisk together 4 tablespoons olive oil, 2 tablespoons
cider vinegar and 2 teaspoons Dijon mustard. Stir in 25 g (1 oz) roasted
chopped hazelnuts, then season with sea salt and black pepper.

variations

tabbouleh

see base recipe page 100

couscous tabbouleh
Prepare the basic recipe, using couscous in place of bulgur wheat. In a bowl, mix 300 ml (10 fl oz) boiling water and ½ teaspoon salt with 200 g (7 oz) quick-cooking couscous, cover and allow to stand for 5 minutes. Fluff with a fork.

quinoa tabbouleh
Prepare the basic recipe, using quinoa in place of bulgur wheat. Boil 500 ml (16 fl oz) water and add 175 g (6 oz) quinoa. Stir, cover and cook for 12 minutes or until the germ separates from the seed. Remove it from heat and allow to stand for about 3 minutes.

tabbouleh with roast peppers
Prepare the basic recipe. Place 1 red and 1 green pepper, halved and seeded, under the grill and cook until the skin is blackened. Place in a paper bag to cool, then peel and slice. Arrange on top of the bulgur salad before serving.

tabbouleh with dukkah
Prepare the basic recipe. In a hot, dry pan, toast 40 g (1½ oz) each of sesame seeds and slivered almonds, 1 tablespoon coriander seeds and 1 teaspoon cumin seeds. Cool, then, using mortar and pestle, coarsely grind seeds and almonds with the salt and pepper. Sprinkle over the top of the bulgur salad.

variations

gado gado

see base recipe page 102

indonesian salad with miso sesame dressing
Prepare the vegetables for the basic salad. Instead of the peanut dressing,
combine 4 tablespoons miso, 6 tablespoons soya sauce, 2 tablespoons sesame
oil, 4 tablespoons rice vinegar and 50 g (2 oz) sesame seeds.

indonesian salad with coconut peanut dressing
Prepare the basic salad and dressing, but when making the dressing, blend
250 ml (8 fl oz) of the water in a blender with 50 g (2 oz) cream of coconut or
flaked coconut, until smooth. Then mix with the remaining water and peanut
butter before adding the remaining ingredients. Serve garnished with dried
flaked coconut.

gado gado with peanuts
Prepare the basic recipe, adding 150 g (5 oz) salted, roasted peanuts with
the tofu.

gado gado with rice
Prepare the basic recipe, using 400 g (14 oz) cooked rice in place of
the potatoes.

variations

whole wheat grain salad

see base recipe page 103

barley salad
Prepare the basic recipe, using barley in place of wheat berries. Dry toast the barley in a heavy-based pan for 3–4 minutes, stirring constantly, then cover with boiling water and simmer for 40 minutes until tender.

whole wheat primavera salad
Prepare the basic recipe, using just 1 pepper and adding 50 g (2 oz) each of blanched sliced carrots, asparagus and broccoli florets. Use basil in place of parsley.

whole wheat, fruit & nut salad
Prepare the whole wheat grains and onion for the basic recipe but omit the peppers. In a frying pan, toast 75 g (3 oz) chopped walnuts and 40 g (1½ oz) each of pumpkin seeds and pine kernels. Toss into the whole wheat grain and onion along with 75 g (3 oz) raisins and the tamari and pepper.

mixed rice salad
Prepare the basic recipe, using 500 g (1 lb 2 oz) cooked mixed rice (a combination of brown, red and wild rice looks stunning) in place of the whole wheat kernels.

variations

avocado & tomato salad

see base recipe page 104

mexican avocado & tomato salad
Prepare the basic recipe, using coriander in place of the basil in the salad and fresh lime juice in place of the balsamic vinegar in the dressing. Add ½–1 tablespoon finely chopped, pickled jalapeño to the salad.

jeweled avocado & tomato salad
Prepare the basic recipe, using mint in place of the basil in the salad and lemon juice in place of the balsamic vinegar in the dressing. Add the seeds of 1 pomegranate to the salad.

avocado & tomato salad boats
Prepare the basic recipe, omitting the avocados when making the salad. Halve and stone the avocados without peeling. To serve, pile the salad into the avocado shells, omit the lettuce, garnish with a lemon wedge and sprinkle with paprika.

'mozzarella' avocado & tomato salad
Prepare the basic recipe, adding 225 g (8 oz) thinly sliced dairy-free 'mozzarella' cheese alternative to the salad ingredients.

warm potato salad

see base recipe page 107

light potato salad
Prepare the basic recipe, omitting the mayonnaise. Replace with a dressing made by combining 2 tablespoons olive oil, juice of 1 lemon, 2 teaspoons wholegrain mustard and salt and pepper to taste.

red, white & blue potato salad
Prepare the basic recipe, using a combination of mixed colours of small red and white potatoes. Purple potatoes can sometimes be found at farmers' markets and grocers which look marvellous too.

german potato salad
Prepare the light potato salad variation above, adding 1 diced dill pickle with the dill and chives. Add 225 g (8 oz) vegan 'hotdog', which has been cooked, cooled and sliced.

cold potato salad
Prepare any of the potato salad recipes, but allow the potatoes and mayonnaise to cool completely before adding the dill and chives. Serve cold.

spinach salad

see base recipe page 108

wilted spinach salad
Prepare the basic recipe, but warm the vinaigrette in a small pan until hot, but not boiling. Pour over the salad and toss to wilt the spinach.

spinach salad with crispy tofu
Prepare the basic recipe. In a large frying pan, heat 2 tablespoons oil over medium heat and add a 350 g (12 oz) block firm tofu, which has been squeezed, drained and cubed. Cook, turning occasionally, until golden brown. Toss into the salad.

spinach salad with toasted pecans
Prepare the basic recipe, but roast 75 g (3 oz) chopped pecans along with the pine kernels.

spinach salad wrap
Prepare the basic recipe and use it to fill four 25-cm (10-inch) flour tortillas. Roll up tightly and fold in the ends. Cut tortillas in half and serve, either cold or heated in a microwave for 1½ minutes until warm.

lentil & rice-stuffed tomatoes

see base recipe page 109

lentil & rice-stuffed peppers
Prepare the basic recipe, using 4 red peppers in place of the tomatoes. Add the flesh of 1 tomato to the lentil and rice stuffing.

tabbouleh-stuffed tomatoes
Prepare the tomatoes as in the basic recipe, but replace the stuffing with tabbouleh (page 100).

lentil & rice-stuffed tomatoes with chickpeas
Prepare the basic recipe, adding 200 g (7 oz) tinned or cooked chickpeas in place of the sweetcorn.

lentil & rice-stuffed tomatoes with vegan 'cheese'
Prepare the basic recipe, adding to the stuffing 125 g (4 oz) chopped vegan 'cheese' alternative – mozzarella-style or Cheddar-style would all work well, depending on availability and your taste preference.

variations

pear & endive salad with caramelised cashews

see base recipe page 110

roast pear & endive salad with caramelised cashews
Prepare the basic recipe, but core the pears and cut into eighths. Place on
parchment paper in an ovenproof dish. Brush or spray with sunflower oil
and roast in the oven at 230°C (450°F/Gas mark 8) for about 10 minutes,
until lightly caramelised. Allow to cool before making the salad.

spinach, pear & endive salad with caramelised cashews
Prepare the basic recipe, using only 3 heads of endive. Do not fan the
endive leaves on the plate; instead, line each plate with baby spinach leaves
(1 package will be sufficient).

orange & endive salad with caramelised cashews
Prepare the basic recipe, using 2 segmented oranges in place of the pears.
Use 1 tablespoon orange juice and 1 tablespoon lemon juice in place of the
vinegar in the dressing.

peach & endive salad with caramelised cashews
Prepare the basic recipe, using 2 large ripe, sliced peaches in place of
the pears.

variations

spring rain salad

see base recipe page 113

japanese sea vegetable salad
Prepare the basic recipe, using a 5-cm (2-inch) piece dried wakami (or other sea vegetable), hydrated, in place of the spring onion. Break 1 sheet toasted nori into smallish pieces and let them fall over the finished salad.

shredded root vegetable salad
Prepare the basic recipe, using 1 carrot, $\frac{1}{2}$ daikon radish and 1 Japanese turnip (Hakurei) or regular turnip, all finely sliced, in place of the cucumber. Marinate the root vegetables in the dressing for at least 1 hour before combining with the other ingredients.

japanese sprout salad
Prepare the basic recipe, using only half of the noodles and adding 200 g (7 oz) bean sprouts. Sprinkle the finished salad with 1 tablespoon toasted sesame seeds.

japanese tofu salad
Prepare the basic salad. Before serving, carefully slice one 350-g (12-oz) block firm tofu, pressed and cut into small cubes and arrange them around the salad.

vegetable dishes

Vegetables can be big and bold, have strong or subtle flavours and come in a range of interesting textures. Mix and match them, experiment with them and you'll find them to be a far cry from the vegetable dishes that were so often dished up before us.

squash & apricot tagine

see variations page 145

This North African specialty is traditionally made in a conical clay pot called a 'tagine', but you can cook it in any pan with a well-fitting lid. Serve with couscous.

1 small courgette, roughly chopped
4 tbsp olive oil
1 onion, finely chopped
2 cloves garlic, crushed
2.5-cm (1-inch) piece root ginger, shredded
$\frac{1}{2}$ tsp ground cumin
$\frac{1}{2}$ tsp ground turmeric
1 tsp paprika
$\frac{1}{2}$ tsp cayenne pepper
1 tsp ground cinnamon
1 medium-large butternut squash, cut into
    chunks

2 medium potatoes, cut into chunks
2 carrots, thickly sliced
125 g (4 oz) French beans, sliced
175 g (6 oz) roughly chopped dried apricots
350 ml (12 fl oz) vegetable stock
2 tsp tomato purée
1 400-g (14-oz) tin chickpeas
2 tsp grated lemon rind
2 tbsp finely chopped fresh parsley
2 tbsp finely chopped fresh coriander
sea salt and black pepper
fresh coriander, to garnish

Place the courgette in a pan of boiling water, simmer for 10 minutes, until very soft, drain and cool. Blend to a smooth purée and set aside. Meanwhile, heat the olive oil in a saucepan, add the onion and cook over medium-high heat for 5 to 7 minutes until it is soft. Add the garlic and ginger and cook for 1 minute, then add the cumin, turmeric, paprika, cayenne and cinnamon. Cook for 1 minute. Stir in the squash, potato, carrots, French beans and apricots until they are coated in the spices. Add the stock and tomato purée and bring to the boil. Cover, reduce the heat and simmer until the squash is tender, about 20 minutes. Add the chickpea, lemon rind, parsley, coriander and the courgette purée. Season to taste with salt and pepper and serve.

Serves 4

spicy spinach & buckwheat crêpes

see variations page 146

These crepes are incredibly versatile and can be filled with a wide range of vegetables, dried beans and nuts. Stuff them with a little leftover stew and you've got a great meal for the family. They are also delicious with sweet fillings such as banana and maple syrup, but add 2 teaspoons of sugar to sweeten the batter. If making crepes for breakfast, make the batter the night before and keep it in the fridge.

for the crepes	for the filling	for the sauce
1 tbsp egg replacer (page 24)	1 kg (2¼ lb) fresh spinach	250 ml (8 fl oz) soya yoghurt
4 tbsp water	2 tbsp rapeseed oil	4 tbsp chopped fresh mint
350 ml (12 fl oz) non-dairy milk	1 medium onion, chopped	2 tsp lime juice
4 tbsp rapeseed oil	4-cm (1¼-inch) ginger, grated	
½ tsp lemon juice	½ tsp whole fennel seeds	
½ tsp salt	4 cardamon pods, grated	
50 g (2 oz) rice flour	½ tsp garam masala	
50 g (2 oz) buckwheat flour	¼ tsp chilli powder	
	½ tsp garam masala	

To make the crepes, whisk together the egg replacer and the water until frothy. Whisk in the other ingredients. Let the batter rest for 30 minutes.

Lightly oil an 22- or 25-cm (8- or 10-inch) cast iron or heavy non-stick frying pan and place over medium-high heat. Once hot, pour in about 2 tablespoons of batter. Swirl it around so it forms a thin layer on the bottom of the pan. If the mixture does not swirl easily, add a little more non-dairy milk to the batter. Cook the crepe and once the top is dry and the underside very lightly browned, flip and cook the other side for 15 to 30 seconds – the

finished crepe should be lightly browned but without crispy edges. Stack the crepes as you make them and keep warm, covered with a clean tea towel. Cook the spinach in just the water clinging to the leaves until it is just tender; drain, cool and roughly chop. Heat the oil in a saucepan, then add the onion and cook for 5 to 7 minutes until it is soft. Add the root ginger and spices and cook for 1 minute. Stir in the spinach and turn to coat in the spices. Preheat the oven to 220°C (425°F/Gas mark 7). Place a generous amount of filling down the centre of each crepe, roll it up, then arrange in an oiled baking dish. Bake for 20 minutes. Meanwhile, combine the sauce ingredients and serve with the crepes. (You can also make and fill the crepes in advance and keep chilled until ready to bake.)

Makes 8–10 crêpes

fennel, pepper & tomato tart

see variations page 147

Shop-bought puff pastry is a gift to vegan cooks, as most major brands are dairy-free, but check before purchasing. This pie is particularly attractive and is a taste sensation.

1 400-g (14-oz) tin kidney beans
2 tbsp non-dairy milk
2 tbsp vegan pesto (page 74)
sea salt and pepper
2 heads fresh fennel
1 red pepper, seeded and halved

6 tomatoes, peeled and thickly sliced
$\frac{1}{2}$ tsp coriander seeds
$\frac{1}{4}$ tsp fennel seeds
2$\frac{1}{2}$ tbsp olive oil
1 tsp lemon juice
1 sheet pre-rolled puff pastry

Preheat oven to 190°C (375°F/Gas mark 5). In a food processor, combine the beans, non-dairy milk and pesto until smooth. Season with salt and pepper. Set aside. Trim the base of the fennel without damaging its ability to hold the bulb together. Remove and discard the green stalks. Cut the fennel into 8 and place in a saucepan. Cover with boiling water and simmer for 10 minutes, drain thoroughly and cool. Meanwhile, place the pepper under a hot grill and cook until the skin blackens, turn and repeat until the whole pepper is charred. Wrap in clingfilm, let cool, then remove the skin and slice. Unwrap the pastry and lay it on greaseproof paper on a baking tray. (If you can't find pastry sheets, roll out pastry into a rectangle 3 mm ($\frac{1}{8}$ inch) thick.) With a knife, score a border 2.5 cm (1 inch) from the edge. This will rise to form the edge of the tart. Spread the bean purée on top of the pastry, taking care to stay within the scored line. Arrange the tomato slices on top, followed by the fennel and pepper. Crush the coriander and fennel seeds and sprinkle over the vegetables with salt and pepper. Brush the outside border with olive oil, then drizzle the remaining oil and lemon juice over the vegetables. Bake for about 25 minutes or until the pastry is risen and golden brown. Slip off the parchment paper and serve warm or at room temperature.
Serves 6

pumpkin & tofu kebabs

see variations page 148

Vegans often feel left out at barbecues. These delicious kebabs provide a tasty solution that will make any vegan feel special. They are easy to prepare and can be made several hours in advance of the party, wrapped in aluminium foil and refrigerated until required.

8 baby potatoes
1 350 g (12-oz) young pumpkin
1 large courgette
2 red, green or yellow peppers, seeded
2 small red onions
8 cherry tomatoes
350 g (12 oz) smoked firm tofu, cut into
    2.5-cm (1-inch) cubes
oil, to brush

for the glaze
125 ml (4 fl oz) olive oil
1$\frac{1}{2}$ tbsp cider or white wine vinegar
2 tbsp maple syrup
2 tbsp orange juice
2 tbsp chopped fresh parsley
1 tbsp chopped fresh rosemary
2 tbsp Dijon mustard

Cook the potatoes in a pan of boiling water until almost cooked; drain and pat dry. Meanwhile, whisk together the ingredients for the glaze. Cut the pumpkin, courgette and pepper into 2.5-cm (1-inch) pieces. Cut the onions into quarters.

Place the potatoes and the vegetables in a shallow dish or container. Pour the marinade over vegetables. Cover and refrigerate for at least 1 hour. Heat the barbeque to medium-high and brush with a little oil. Alternately thread the vegetables and tofu onto 8 skewers, leaving a little space between each. Place the skewers on the rack and cook, turning frequently and basting with the marinade for about 10 minutes. Remove when the pumpkin and courgette are tender-crisp.

Serves 4

potato & mushroom filo pie

see variations page 149

Filo pastry is marvellous – it feels like an indulgent treat, but it is low in fat, looks sophisticated, yet is simple to use. The trick is to work quickly to prevent it from drying out, while keeping unused sheets either covered in wax paper or a damp cloth. (More tips on working with filo on page 15.) If you wish, this dish may be prepared in advance, covered in clingfilm and kept refrigerated until you're ready to cook it.

675 g (1½ lb) floury potatoes, such as King
    Edwards or Maris Piper, thinly sliced
1 tbsp olive oil
2 onions, finely sliced
225 g (8 oz) chestnut mushrooms, sliced
1 tsp dried dill
1 tbsp arrowroot
250 ml (8 fl oz) soya cream
125 ml (4 fl oz) vegetable stock

1 tbsp nutritional yeast
1 bunch spring onions, sliced
pinch paprika
pinch ground nutmeg
sea salt and black pepper
6 sheets filo pastry
olive oil, to brush
sesame seeds, to sprinkle

Preheat oven to 190°C (375°F/Gas mark 5). Oil an 28x18-cm (11x7-inch) baking dish. In a large pan of boiling water, blanch the potato slices for 2 minutes, plunge into cold water, drain and blot off excess water with a tea towel or kitchen paper. Heat the oil in a frying pan, add the onions and cook over medium-high heat for 5 to 7 minutes or until soft. Add the mushrooms and cook until just wilted, then stir in the dill. Mix the arrowroot with 2 tablespoons of the soya cream, then stir in the remaining soya cream, stock and nutritional yeast. In the prepared dish, layer the potatoes, onion-mushroom mixture and spring onions, sprinkling a little of the cream mixture, paprika, nutmeg, salt and pepper over each potato layer. Pour the remaining cream mixture over the top layer. Working quickly, cut the filo

slightly larger than the baking dish. Place the first sheet on top of the vegetables, tuck the overlap down inside the dish, then brush with olive oil. Repeat until all the sheets are used. Brush the top generously with oil and sprinkle with sesame seeds. Score the pastry into portions. Bake for 20 to 25 minutes, until golden; test that the potatoes are cooked by inserting a knife through the scored pastry.

Serves 4

winter vegetable bake

see variations page 150

Root vegetables make a star appearance in this one-pot wonder.

2 tbsp olive oil
2 red onions, cut into wedges
½ butternut squash, diced
½ swede, diced
3 medium carrots, thickly
   sliced
2 medium leeks, sliced
2 medium parsnips, thickly
   sliced
3 raw beets, quartered

2 celery sticks, sliced
1 tsp caraway seeds
2 cloves of garlic, crushed
3 tbsp tomato purée
300 ml (10 fl oz) vegetable
   stock
1 400-g (14-oz) tin chopped
   tomatoes
1 tsp mixed dried herbs
sea salt and pepper

1 tbsp cornflour
1 tbsp water
for the savoury scones
225 g (8 oz) flour
1 tbsp baking powder
½ tsp salt
1 tsp dried rosemary
50 g (2 oz) soya margarine
185 ml (6 fl oz) soya milk
soya milk, to glaze

Heat the oil in a heavy-duty, flameproof casserole, then add the onions, squash, swede, carrots, leeks, parsnips, beet, celery, caraway seeds and garlic. Cook over medium–high heat for 5–7 minutes or until onions are soft. Add the tomato purée, stock, chopped tomatoes and their juices and herbs. Season to taste. Bring to the boil, cover and simmer for 30 minutes. Stir the cornflour into the water, then pour mixture into the pan, stirring, until the liquid thickens. Meanwhile, to make the scones, place all the dry ingredients into a bowl. Rub in the margarine with your fingertips or a fork, until the mixture resembles fine breadcrumbs. Add soya milk and stir until a soft, smooth dough is formed, adding more flour if the dough is sticky. Roll out dough 2 cm (½ inch) thick on a floured surface and stamp out 8 to 9 rounds with a 4-cm (2-inch) cookie cutter. Preheat the oven to 200°C (400°F/Gas mark 6). Arrange the scones around the edge of the vegetable mixture, brush the tops with soya milk and bake for 20–25 minutes or until scones have risen and are golden brown.
Serves 4–6

mediterranean warm roast vegetable wrap

see variations page 151

These deeply satisfying warm wraps are equally good when served cold. Try them as a lunchbox meal. Simply allow the vegetables to fully cool before constructing the wrap.

1 tbsp olive oil
1 clove of garlic, crushed
sea salt and black pepper, to taste
1 red pepper, seeded and cut into strips
1 green pepper, seeded and cut into strips
1 small courgette, cut into strips
1 small yellow squash, seeded and cut
   into strips

185 g (6 oz) cherry tomatoes
1–2 tsp balsamic vinegar
225 g (8 oz) hummus
4 tortillas, warmed
125 g (4 oz) baby spinach leaves, washed
   and dried

Preheat oven to 220°C (425°F/Gas mark 7). In a bowl, combine the oil, garlic, salt and pepper. Lay all the vegetables in an oiled roasting tin, pour in the oil mixture and toss, taking care to coat each strip. Bake, turning once, until the vegetables are slightly charred and tender, about 40 minutes. Sprinkle with a little balsamic vinegar to taste. Cool slightly; the vegetables should be warm, not hot.

Spread the hummus on the warmed tortillas, lay the raw spinach on the hummus and top with the roasted vegetables. Roll up the tortillas and tuck in the ends. Serve immediately.

Serves 4

pepperoncini & tofu sandwiches

see variations page 152

This is a great sandwich. It works well with leftover tofu and is good with toasted or untoasted bread. Use roast peppers if pepperoncini are unavailable.

1 tsp sunflower oil
125 g (4 oz) firm tofu, pressed and drained, cut
    into thick slices
$^1/_2$ ripe avocado, sliced
$1^1/_2$ tsp lemon juice
4 tbsp nondairy mayonnaise

4 slices wholemeal sandwich bread
1 large tomato
3 small pepperoncini peppers, stems removed
    and sliced lengthwise
baby lettuce leaves
sea salt and black pepper

Heat a heavy frying pan until very hot. Add the oil, then the tofu slices. Cook over medium-high heat until golden brown on both sides.

Toss the avocado in $^1/_2$ teaspoon lemon juice. Combine the mayonnaise with the remaining lemon juice. Spread the mayonnaise over the bread and top with the tofu, avocado, tomato, pepperoncini and lettuce. Season each sandwich with salt and pepper.

Makes 2 sandwiches

mixed vegetable stirfry

see variations page 153

How could something so wonderful take so little time to prepare! Just select your noodles with care. Most are fine, but some may contain eggs or butter. Also, watch out for 'lactose' on the ingredients list.

225 g (8 oz) rice or wheat noodles
1 tbsp peanut or vegetable oil
1 red chilli pepper, sliced
1 clove of garlic, sliced
500 g (1 lb 2 oz) mixed fresh vegetables such as bok choy, snow peas, baby sweetcorn and broccoli florets

2 tbsp soya sauce
2½ tbsp sweet chilli sauce
200 g (7 oz) bean sprouts
2 tsp sesame oil

Cook the noodles according to package directions; drain.

Meanwhile, heat the oil in a large frying pan or wok and fry the chilli and garlic for 1 minute. Add the mixed vegetables and stirfry over high heat for 3 minutes. Add the soya sauce and chilli sauce and toss to coat. Add the bean sprouts and continue to stirfry 2 to 3 minutes until the vegetables are tender-crisp. Toss with the noodles and drizzle with the sesame oil; serve immediately.

Serves 4

quick green vegetable curry

see variations page 154

Here's an ideal supper dish suitable for friends or family. Don't feel restricted by the selection of vegetables. Use what is readily available or try using vegetables such as baby aubergines, okra, bok choy or sprouting broccoli. Serve with a chapati or with rice.

2 tbsp sunflower oil
1 medium onion, chopped
1 courgette, sliced
2 tbsp grated root ginger
2 cloves of garlic, crushed
1–2 green chillies, seeded and chopped
2 tsp ground cumin
½ tsp ground turmeric
½ tsp ground coriander

350 g (12 oz) fresh broccoli, cut into florets
175 g (6 oz) fresh or frozen French beans
175 g (6 oz) frozen peas
350 ml (12 fl oz) coconut milk
250 ml (8 fl oz) vegetable stock
sea salt
225 g (8 oz) fresh baby spinach leaves
4 tablespoons chopped fresh coriander
200 ml (7 fl oz) soya yoghurt

Heat the oil in a saucepan, add the onion and cook over medium-high heat for 3 minutes. Stir in the courgette and cook for another 3 minutes or until the onion is soft. Stir in the root ginger, garlic, chillies and spices and cook for 1 minute.

Add the broccoli, beans, peas, coconut milk and stock. Bring to the boil, reduce the heat, cover and simmer for about 6 minutes, until the broccoli is just cooked. Season to taste with salt. Stir in the spinach and coriander. When the spinach is wilted, stir in the yoghurt, heat through without boiling and serve.

Serves 4

antipasto pizza

see variations page 155

This pizza is constructed from the wonderful Italian ingredients that come in jars. There is a huge selection. Try white asparagus, mushrooms, capers or mixed antipasto. Avoid using commercial pizza sauce – it's way too salty. Prepared pizza bases generally do not contain any prohibited ingredients, but do check the ingredients before purchasing.

1 prepared 30-cm (12-inch) pizza base
1 tbsp tomato purée
3 tbsp vegan pesto (page 74)
200 ml (7 fl oz) tomato sauce
black pepper
75 g (3 oz) sun-dried tomatoes in oil,
    drained and sliced

4 artichoke hearts from a jar, quartered
2 roasted red peppers from jar, cut into 1.5-cm
    (1/2-inch) strips
12 black olives

Preheat oven to 220°C (425°F/Gas mark 7).

Arrange the pizza base on a baking tray. Spread with the tomato purée, then with the pesto. Spread with the tomato sauce and season with pepper. Sprinkle evenly all over with the tomatoes, artichoke hearts, peppers and olives.

Bake pizza until the crust browns, about 10 minutes.

Makes 1 pizza

courgette fritters with tzatziki

see variations page 156

These fritters use both spelt and rice flours. If these are unavailable, use wholemeal, plain or even buckwheat flour – or a combination of flours.

for the tzatziki
350 ml (12 fl oz) soya yoghurt
1 tbsp olive oil
½ cucumber, shredded
1 clove garlic, crushed
1 tsp chopped fresh dill or ½ tsp dried dill
sea salt and black pepper
for the fritters
125 g (4 oz) rice flour
125 g (4 oz) spelt flour
1 tsp baking powder

25 g (1 oz) quick-cooking oats
2 tbsp nutritional yeast
2 tbsp chopped fresh mint or 1 tsp dried mint
1 tsp ground coriander
2 medium courgette, coarsely shredded
3 spring onions, finely chopped
1 red chilli pepper, finely chopped
sea salt and black pepper
125 ml (4 fl oz) soya yoghurt
rapeseed oil, to fry

In a small bowl, combine all the sauce ingredients. Chill. In a bowl, combine the flours, baking powder, oats, yeast, mint and coriander. Place the courgette in a clean tea towel and squeeze out excess liquid, then add to the flour mixture, tossing to coat. Add the spring onions, red chilli and salt and pepper to taste. Gently stir in the yoghurt, adding a little water if the mixture feels too dry. Set aside for 10 minutes for the baking powder to begin to activate. Heat a frying pan or griddle until very hot, then coat with a little oil. Using about half a ladleful of fritter batter, drop the batter onto the hot frying pan and spread out with a spatula. Cook until bubbles rise to the surface of the fritter and the base is golden brown. Turn and cook the other side. Remove and keep warm while you make the remaining fritters. Serve with tzatziki.
Serves 4

malay laksa & tofu puffs

see variations page 157

Deep-fried tofu puffs are popular in Southeast Asia and are good with any Asian-style stew.

1 tbsp sunflower oil
2 heads bok choy, sliced
2 medium carrots, thinly sliced on diagonal
2 celery sticks, thinly sliced on diagonal
125 g (4 oz) baby sweetcorn, cut down the centre lengthwise
2 cloves of garlic, finely sliced
2 5-cm (2-inch) pieces root ginger, shredded
1 l (1¾ pt) vegetable stock
1 400-ml (14 fl oz) tin coconut milk
3 tbsp tamari
2 tbsp red curry paste

1–2 tsp sambel oelek or another chilli paste
1 7.5-g (¼-oz) sachet instant miso soup powder
2 stalks lemongrass, smashed
2 sprigs laksa leaves (Vietnamese mint), if available or 1 tsp dried mint
sea salt
500 g (1 lb) firm tofu, pressed, drained and cut into 2.5-cm (1-inch) pieces
oil for deep frying
125 g (4 oz) rice vermicelli noodles
200 g (7 oz) bean sprouts
1 lime, quartered, to garnish

Heat the oil in a wok or saucepan and stirfry the bok choy until wilted. Remove and set aside. In the same saucepan, place the carrot, celery, corn, garlic and ginger. Stirfry until hot. Add the stock, coconut milk, tamari, curry paste, chilli sauce, miso soup powder, mint, lemongrass and laksa sprigs or mint. Season. Simmer for 15 minutes. Remove lemongrass and laksa stalks (the leaves may remain). While stew is cooking, prepare the tofu. Heat oil to 190°C (375°F) in a wok or deep fryer. Deep-fry the tofu in batches until golden brown and puffed. Drain and keep warm. Meanwhile, place the noodles in a bowl, cover with boiling water and soak for 5 minutes. Drain and divide between 4 bowls. Return bok choy to the saucepan with the bean sprouts and heat through, pour over the noodles, top with the tofu and serve with a slice of lime.

Serves 4

variations

squash & apricot tagine

see base recipe page 125

mixed vegetable & apricot tagine
Prepare the basic recipe, using 1 kg (2¼ lb) chopped vegetables such as pumpkin, parsnip, sweet potato and cabbage or kale in place of the squash.

bean & apple tagine
Prepare the basic recipe, using dried apples in place of the apricots and tinned broad beans in place of the chickpea.

squash & prune tagine
Prepare the basic recipe, using quartered dried prunes in place of the apricots.

squash & apricot tagine with chermoula
Prepare the basic recipe and serve with a side dish of chermoula. Mix together 125 ml (4 fl oz) lemon juice, 180 ml (6 fl oz) olive oil, 50 g (2 oz) finely chopped fresh coriander, 4 tablespoons finely chopped fresh flat-leaf parsley, 2 crushed cloves of garlic, pinch each of paprika and cayenne. Season with salt.

variations

spicy spinach & buckwheat crêpes

see base recipe page 126

spicy spinach & chickpea buckwheat crêpes with minted yoghurt
Prepare the basic recipe, adding a 400-g (14-oz) tin chickpeas with
the spinach.

spicy spinach French-style crêpes with minted yoghurt
Prepare the basic recipe, using 125 g (4 oz) plain flour in place of
rice and buckwheat flours. Or, use 60 g (2 oz) each of plain flour and
wholemeal flour.

oven-roast vegetable crêpes
Prepare the basic recipe, using the roasted vegetables from the
Mediterranean Warm Vegetable Wrap (page 134) in place of the spicy
spinach. Serve with the minted yoghurt sauce, if desired.

creamy mushroom crêpes
Prepare the basic recipe, using the mushroom filling from the Mushroom
Lasagna (page 196) in place of the spinach. Omit the yoghurt sauce.

variations

fennel, pepper & tomato tart

see base recipe page 128

roast asparagus & tomato tart

Prepare the basic recipe, using 500 g (1 lb 2 oz) asparagus, trimmed (the thinner varieties work best) in place of the fennel and pepper. Arrange the asparagus spears in a row, tips in alternate directions, to ensure everyone gets their share of tips and bases.

leek, tomato & dill tart

Prepare the basic recipe, using 4 leeks, white parts only, in place of the fennel and peppers. Sweat in a covered pan with 1 tablespoon olive oil and 1 teaspoon dried dill tips for 5 minutes, then cool before arranging on top of the tomatoes.

mushroom, tomato & thyme tart

Prepare the basic recipe, using 4 large Portobello mushrooms, thickly sliced, in place of the fennel and peppers. Cook in 2 tablespoons olive oil with 1 teaspoon dried thyme until just wilted and the liquid has evaporated, then cool before arranging on top of the tomatoes.

roast vegetable tart

Prepare the basic recipe, using the roasted vegetables from the Mediterranean Warm Vegetable Wrap (page 134) in place of the tomatoes, pepper and fennel.

variations

pumpkin & tofu kebabs

see base recipe page 129

shiitake mushroom kebabs with maple-mustard glaze
Prepare the basic recipe, using 16 shiitake mushrooms in place of the
pumpkin and courgette. Steam the mushrooms for 2 minutes prior to
preparation to reduce risk of them splitting and falling off the skewer.

butternut squash kebabs with maple-mustard glaze
Prepare the basic recipe, using butternut squash in place of the pumpkin.
Parboil the butternut squash with the potatoes.

aubergine kebabs with maple-mustard glaze
Prepare the basic recipe, using aubergine in place of the pumpkin.
To prepare, cut a small aubergine into 2.5-cm (1-inch) cubes and
sprinkle with salt. Rest for 30 minutes, then wipe away the bitter
juices with kitchen paper.

pumpkin & tofu kebabs with adobo glaze
Prepare the basic kebabs, but in place of the maple mustard glaze combine
1–2 tablespoons chopped tinned chipotle chilli, 1 tablespoon adobo sauce
(from tin), 4 tablespoons each of agave nectar and freshly squeezed
mandarin orange juice and 1 tablespoon cider vinegar.

potato & mushroom filo pie

see base recipe page 130

potato & mushroom puff pastry pie
Prepare the basic recipe, using puff pastry in place of the filo.

potato, pea & tomato filo pie
Prepare the basic recipe, but use 200 g (7 oz) cooked frozen peas and 2 large peeled, seeded and chopped tomatoes mixed together in place of the cooked mushrooms.

sweet potato & sweetcorn filo pie
Prepare the basic recipe, replacing half of the potatoes with sweet potatoes and using 300 g (11 oz) cooked frozen sweetcorn in place of the cooked mushrooms.

caramelised onion & potato filo pie
Prepare the basic recipe, omitting the onions, mushrooms and spring onions. Instead, cook 500 g (1 lb 2 oz) sliced onions in 4 tablespoons olive oil over a very low heat for about 30 minutes, stirring often. Stir in 1 tablespoon sugar, then continue to cook for 10 to 15 minutes until golden brown. Add the dill and proceed as with the basic recipe.

variations

winter vegetable bake

see base recipe page 133

spicy bean & vegetable bake

Prepare the basic recipe, but omit the beetroot and add 1 400-g (14-oz) tin kidney or butter beans and 1–2 teaspoons hot chilli sauce.

roast winter vegetable bake

Instead of the basic recipe, place all the vegetables in a roasting pan and toss with olive oil. Bake in the oven at 220°C (425°F/Gas mark 7) until just beginning to char on the edges, about 50 minutes. Place in a frying pan and add the tomato purée, stock, tomatoes and juices and herbs. Season to taste. Bring to the boil and simmer, uncovered, for 15 minutes. Continue as with the basic recipe.

apple & pear bake

Instead of the basic recipe, peel, core and chop 3 pears and 3 cooking apples, then toss with 185 g (6 oz) sugar and ½ teaspoon cinnamon and ¼ teaspoon nutmeg. Place in an ovenproof dish and sprinkle with 3 tablespoons water. Top with the basic scone mixture, adding 2 tablespoons sugar and omitting rosemary and bake as in the basic recipe.

variations

mediterranean warm roast vegetable wrap

see base recipe page 134

warm roast aubergine wrap
Prepare the basic recipe, replacing the courgette and squash with 1 aubergine, which has been cut into strips, salted, allowed to stand and patted dry.

indonesian wrap
Prepare the basic recipe, using 1 tablespoon soya sauce in place of the balsamic vinegar and spreading the tortillas with peanut satay sauce (page 102) in place of the hummus.

high-protein mediterranean wrap
Prepare the basic recipe, adding half a soya-based 'chicken' cutlet or sliced smoked or flavoured tempeh, to each wrap. Cook the cutlet or tempeh according to the manufacturer's instructions.

'mozzarella' mediterranean wrap
Prepare the basic recipe, adding 4 slices Mozzarella-style dairy-free 'cheese' to each wrap.

variations

pepperoncini & tofu sandwiches

see base recipe page 136

pepperoncini & tapenade sandwiches
Prepare the basic recipe, omitting the tofu. Spread 1 tablespoon tapenade (page 85) on each sandwich on top of the avocado slices.

tofu & chilli jam sandwiches
Prepare the basic recipe, using 1 tablespoon red chilli jam per sandwich in place of the pepperoncini.

pepperoncini & falafal sandwiches
Prepare the basic recipe, using 2 or 3 falafal balls, sliced in thirds, in place of the tofu.

tofu & horseradish sandwiches
Prepare the basic recipe, omitting the pepperoncini and adding ½ to 1 tablespoon prepared horseradish to the mayonnaise.

mixed vegetable stirfry

see base recipe page 137

quick mushroom stirfry
Prepare the basic recipe, replacing the mixed vegetables with
50 g (2 oz) each of sliced chestnut mushrooms, sliced oyster or
shiitake mushrooms, mangetout and 1 sliced head bok choy.

quick stirfry with bamboo shoots & water chestnuts
Prepare the basic recipe, replacing the mixed vegetables with half
a 225-g (8-oz) can each of bamboo shoots and water chestnuts, 50 g (2 oz)
mangetout and 1 sliced head bok choy.

mixed vegetable stirfry with cashews
Prepare the basic recipe, adding 150 g (5 oz) roasted, unsalted cashews with
the bean sprouts.

mixed vegetable stirfry with black bean sauce
Prepare the basic recipe, using black bean sauce in place of the sweet
chilli sauce.

variations

green vegetable curry

see base recipe page 138

quick vegetable lentil curry
Prepare the basic recipe, adding 1 400-g (14-oz) tin drained lentils with the spinach and yoghurt.

thai green vegetable curry
Prepare the basic recipe, using 2 tablespoons Thai curry paste in place of the cumin, turmeric and coriander.

vegetable curry with marinated tofu
Prepare the basic recipe, adding marinated tofu with the yoghurt. To make it, at least an hour before preparation, press, drain and slice the tofu. Cover with a marinade made from 1 tablespoon each of curry powder, cornflour, lemon juice and water. After 1 hour marinating, drain the tofu and discard marinade. Stirfry the tofu in oil. Prepare the basic recipe and add the tofu with the yoghurt.

variations

antipasto pizza

see base recipe page 141

antipasto pizza with 'cheese'
Prepare the basic recipe, top with slices of vegan Mozzarella 'cheese' and sprinkle with vegan 'Parmesan' (page 22 or purchased) before baking.

antipasto pizza with smoked tofu
Prepare the basic recipe, top with 125 g (4 oz) shredded smoked tofu.

antipasto ciabatta pizza
Cut 2 ciabatta in half lengthwise to use as the base, then continue as for the basic recipe.

polenta pizza
Make 90 g (3 oz) quick-cooking polenta according to the package directions. Spread the mixture on 2 oiled and lined 20-cm (8-inch) cake tins and bake until firm, about 12 minutes. Use as pizza bases; continue as for basic recipe.

variations

courgette fritters with tzatziki

see base recipe page 142

carrot fritters with tzatziki
Prepare the basic recipe, using 225 g (8 oz) carrots in place of courgette (there is no need to squeeze the liquid out of the carrots).

sweetcorn fritters with tzatziki
Prepare the basic recipe, using 300 g (11 oz) frozen or tinned sweetcorn in place of the courgette (there is no need to squeeze the liquid out of the corn). Use parsley in place of mint.

parsnip fritters with tzatziki
Prepare the basic recipe, replacing courgette with 225 g (8 oz) grated parsnips, which have been blanched in boiling water for 2 minutes, then drained and squeezed dry. Use sage in place of mint.

courgette fritters with tahini sauce
Prepare the basic fritters, but replace tzatziki with tahini sauce. Combine 1 crushed clove of garlic, 75 g (3 oz) tahini, 4 tablespoons each of lemon juice and soya yoghurt and 1 teaspoon freshly chopped parsley. Season to taste with a little sea salt, a pinch of cayenne pepper and a few drops of agave nectar.

variations

malay laksa with tofu puffs

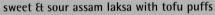

see base recipe page 144

sweet & sour assam laksa with tofu puffs
Prepare the basic recipe, but mix a little of the stock into 4 tablespoons tamarind to create a smooth paste and add the paste to the stew with the remaining stock.

laksa with flavoured noodles & tofu puffs
Prepare the basic recipe, using flavoured rice noodles such as pumpkin and ginger rice noodles, green tea or buckwheat noodles in place of the vermicelli noodles.

laksa with skiitake, sea vegetables & tofu puffs
Prepare the basic recipe, using 125 g (4 oz) shiitake mushroom cut into thick slices in place of the celery. Add 1 piece kombu (kelp) about 5 cm (4 inches) long with the lemongrass; discard it at the same time. Garnish with toasted nori pieces and the tofu puffs.

pumpkin & sweetcorn laksa with tofu puffs
Prepare the basic recipe, using 350 g (12 oz) pumpkin or butternut squash, cut into chunks and 125 g (4 oz) baby sweetcorn, cut in half lengthwise, in place of the bok choy, carrots and celery.

bean, lentil &
nutty dishes

Beans, lentils and nuts love bold flavours making

them perfect in dishes loaded with spices or when

combined with rich sauces. They also shine in

combination with the zingy flavour of fruit. Some

dishes here benefit from slow cooking while others

can be rustled up in no time.

refried bean tacos

see variations page 176

Making your own tacos is the one way to be sure that you're getting a truly vegan taco.
The 'cheese' here is optional for those who seek authenticity!

11 tbsp sunflower oil
1 small onion, sliced
1 400-g (14-oz) tin vegetarian refried beans
1 113-g (4-oz) tin chopped green
    chillies, drained
4 tinned plum tomatoes
12 black olives, halved
125 g (4 oz) non-dairy Cheddar-style 'cheese'
12 cornmeal tacos shells, warmed

for the topping
shredded lettuce
soya yoghurt or non-dairy sour cream
chopped fresh tomatoes
chopped onion
chopped fresh coriander

Heat the oil in a frying pan, add the onion and cook over medium-high heat for
5 to 7 minutes or until the onion is soft. Reduce the heat, then stir in the refried beans,
green chillies, tomatoes and olives. Bring the mixture to a boil, stirring constantly to prevent
the beans from scorching. Stir in the 'cheese', if using.

Place the bean mixture into the warmed taco shells and serve with a selection of
the toppings.

Serves 4

three bean chilli

see variations page 177

Here's comfort food and one that is always a hit with meat-eaters too. Make this recipe in bulk for parties or potluck dinners or freeze it in meal-sized portions. It improves with keeping, so it is a great dish to prepare ahead of time.

2 tbsp sunflower oil
1 large onion, chopped
3 carrots, chopped
2 green peppers, seeded and chopped
3 cloves of garlic, crushed
2–4 tbsp chilli powder or to taste
1 tsp smoked paprika
1 tsp ground cumin
1 400-g (14-oz) tin kidney beans
1 400-g (14-oz) tin pinto beans
1 400-g (14-oz) tin black beans

2 400-g (14 oz) tins chopped tomatoes
1 113-g (4-oz) tin green chillies, chopped and drained
1 100-g (3½-oz) tin tomato purée
125 g (3½ oz) quartered button mushrooms
300 g (9 oz) frozen or tinned sweetcorn
1 tbsp dried oregano
2 tsp unsweetened cocoa powder
750 ml (2¼ pt) vegetable stock or beer
1 tsp sugar
sea salt

Heat the oil in a saucepan, then add the onion and cook for 5 to 7 minutes until the onion is soft. Add the carrots, peppers and garlic and cook for 3 minutes. Add the chilli powder, smoked paprika and cumin, then cook for another minute. Stir in all the remaining ingredients. Bring to the boil, then reduce the heat and simmer for at least 20 minutes. Alternatively, bake at 180°C (350°F/Gas mark 4) for 20 minutes. The chilli matures with longer cooking.

Serves 6–8

pasta e fagioli

see variations page 178

Some call it a stew, others a soup, but either way this dish makes a wholesome meal. It is a good recipe to cook in bulk for a crowd.

2 tbsp olive oil
1 medium onion, finely chopped
1 small carrot, finely chopped
1 stalk celery, finely chopped
4 large cloves garlic, chopped
350 g (12-oz) bottled passata or 1 400-g
    (14-oz) tin chopped tomotoes
1.5 l (2¹/₂ pt) vegetable stock

2 sprigs rosemary, left intact or 2 tsp
    dried rosemary
1 large sprig thyme, left intact or 1 tsp
    dried thyme
1 large fresh bay leaf or 2 dried bay leaves
300 g (11 oz) ditalini or other small pasta
2 400-g (14-oz) tins borlotti beans
sea salt and black pepper

Heat the oil in a frying pan, then add the onion, carrot and celery. Cook over medium-high heat for 5 to 7 minutes or until the onion is soft. Stir in the garlic, passata or tomatoes, stock and herbs. Bring to the boil. Reduce the heat, cover and simmer for 30 minutes, stirring occasionally.

Return the stew to a rapid boil and add the pasta and beans. Reduce the heat to medium and cook for 6 to 8 minutes, until the pasta is just cooked. Remove the herb sprigs, if using and the bay leaf before serving.

Serves 6

hippie hotpot

see variations page 179

The traditional Lancashire hotpot consists of lamb, onions and potatoes layered in a heavy pot and slow-cooked all day. This 'hippie' version uses lentils in place of the meat, but is just as fine and filling as its ancestor.

200 g (7 oz) red lentils, washed
600 ml (1 pt) vegetable stock
2 small carrots, chopped
1 parsnip, chopped
1 bay leaf
1 200-g (7-oz) tin chopped tomatoes

1 tsp dried mixed herbs
1 tbsp nutritional yeast
sea salt and black pepper
2 medium onions, sliced in rings
700 g (1½ lb) potatoes, sliced
olive oil for brushing

Preheat oven to 150°C (325°F/Gas mark 3).

Place the lentils in a saucepan with the stock, carrots, parsnip and bay leaf. Bring to the boil, cover and simmer for 15 to 20 minutes until the lentils are soft and the vegetables are cooked. Discard the bay leaf. Stir in the tomatoes, herbs and nutritional yeast, then season to taste with salt and pepper.

Arrange the lentil mix, onions and potatoes in layers, sprinkling a little pepper and salt over each potato layer and finishing with a layer of potatoes. Brush the top generously with oil and bake for about 1½ hours or until the top is browned and the potatoes are tender.

Serves 4

lentil & quinoa burgers with mango salsa

see variations page 180

These lentil and quinoa burgers have a good texture and go well in a bap or served on their own with the salsa and a green salad. They are quite delicate to handle, but they will firm up if allowed to chill before cooking.

200 g (7 oz) green or brown
    lentils
125 g (3½ oz) quinoa
1 tbsp olive oil
1 small onion, finely chopped
1 small carrot, grated
2 tsp ground cumin
40 g (1½ oz) breadcrumbs
2 tbsp chopped fresh parsley
3 tbsp tomato purée

1 tbsp soya sauce
1 tbsp nutritional yeast
2 tbsp peanut butter
sea salt and black pepper
cornmeal or oats, for coating
olive oil, for frying
for the mango salsa
1 mango, peeled and chopped
1 medium green pepper,
    seeded and chopped

1 small red onion, finely
    chopped
1 jalapeño pepper, finely
    chopped
2 tbsp lime juice
1 tbsp pineapple juice or
    orange juice
sea salt and black pepper
chopped fresh coriander,
    to garnish

Put the lentils and quinoa in a saucepan of boiling water, reduce the heat and simmer until soft, approximately 20 minutes. Drain and cool and then use a potato masher to break down the lentils.

To make the salsa, combine all the ingredients in a bowl and set aside.

Meanwhile, heat the oil in a frying pan, add the onion and cook over a medium-high heat for 5–7 minutes or until it is soft. Stir in the carrots and cumin and cook for 2 minutes.

Combine the lentil-quinoa mixture with the onions and carrots. Stir in the breadcrumbs, parsley, tomato paste, soya sauce, nutritional yeast and peanut butter. Knead the mixture with your hands until it sticks together. Form the mixture into 8 burgers. Coat each burger in a little cornmeal or oats. Chill, if desired, until ready to cook. To serve, heat 1 tablespoon olive oil in a frying pan and fry the burgers over a medium-low heat until crisp and golden on each side, 4–5 minutes. Serve with the mango salsa.

Serves 4

tomato farinata

see variations page 181

This northern Italian treat is not a pancake, not a frittata, not a tortilla, although it has the qualities of all three. You do have to think ahead to prepare the batter, which needs a couple of hours to rest, but once you start cooking, it is quick and simple to prepare. Try it cold, cut into squares for an unusual picnic treat. Gram flour is made from chickpeas and is available in the ethnic section of some large supermarkets, most whole-food shops and always at Asian grocery shops.

for the farinata
250 g (9 oz) gram (chickpea) flour
1 tsp sea salt
450 ml (¾ pt) warm water
4 tbsp olive oil
black pepper

for the topping
2 ripe tomatoes, skinned, seeded and chopped
2 spring onions, sliced
4 black olives, quartered
½ tsp red pepper flakes (optional)
1 tbsp chopped fresh rosemary
1 tsp lemon juice
sea salt and black pepper

Sift the gram flour into a bowl, add the salt. Pour in the water, stirring constantly, to form a thin smooth batter. Cover with a damp cloth and let rest in a warm place for at least 2 hours. Preheat oven to 220°C (425°F/Gas mark 7). Gently stir 3 tablespoons of the olive oil into the batter. Place the remaining oil in an 20x20-cm (8x8-inch) baking tin, then place the pan in the oven briefly until the oil is very hot. Pour in the batter and arrange the topping ingredients on the surface, sprinkling the surface evenly with each in turn. Bake for about 15 minutes, until golden and crisp. Serve hot or at room temperature.

Serves 4

hungarian nut loaf

see variations page 182

Not the usual heavy nut roast but a lighter-textured loaf that uses lentils as well as nuts. The tomato-pimento sauce adds moisture and flavour.

200 g (7 oz) red lentils, rinsed
625 ml (1 pt) vegetable stock
1 bay leaf
1½ tbsp olive oil
1 large onion, finely chopped
1 leek, white part only, finely chopped
1 red pepper, seeded and chopped
125 g (4 oz) chestnut or button mushrooms, finely chopped

2 medium carrots, grated
125 g (4 oz) whole Brazil nuts, toasted and chopped
1 clove of garlic, crushed
1 tbsp lemon juice
1 tbsp tomato purée
1 tbsp paprika
1 tsp caraway seeds
3 tbsp nutritional yeast
90 g (3½ oz) wholemeal breadcrumbs
2 tbsp chopped fresh parsley

sea salt and black pepper
for the tomato-pimento sauce
1 tbsp tomato purée
1 tsp paprika
1 400-g (14-oz) tin chopped tomatoes
2 tinned pimentos, drained and chopped
150 ml (¼ pt) red wine or vegetable stock
1 tsp dried sage
sea salt and black pepper

Preheat the oven to 190°C (375°F/Gas mark 5). Oil and line a 23x13-cm (2-pint) loaf tin with parchment paper. Put the lentils in a saucepan with the bouillon and bay leaf. Bring to the boil, cover and simmer for about 15 minutes until the lentils are soft. Discard the bay leaf.

Heat the oil in a saucepan, add the onion and cook over a medium-high heat for 5–7 minutes or until the onion is soft. Set aside half the onion for the sauce. To the remaining onion, add the leek, red pepper, mushrooms and carrot. Cook for 5 minutes longer. Add all the remaining ingredients. Press the mixture into the prepared tin and bake for 60 minutes, until a toothpick inserted into the centre comes out clean. If the top is overcooking,

cover with aluminium foil halfway though the cooking time. Leave to cool for 10 minutes before removing from the tin. To make the sauce, put the reserved onion and remaining sauce ingredients, except the parsley, into a pan. Bring to the boil, then reduce the heat and simmer for 15 minutes. Serve with the loaf.

Serves 6–8

vegetable mole oaxaca

see variations page 183

Every family in Mexico has their own way of preparing this fabulous dish, which originated in Oaxaca, so feel free to experiment with the recipe. Use your favourite chillies, vegetables and beans or add raisins or almonds.

40 g (1½ oz) toasted pumpkin seeds or blanched almonds
1 400-g (14-oz) tin chopped tomatoes
4 tbsp tahini
1 tbsp sunflower oil
1 onion, finely chopped
2 cloves garlic, crushed
1 green pepper, seeded and chopped
1 large plantain, sliced

1 small butternut squash, chopped
2 medium potatoes, cut into chunks
1 jalapeño, green or scotch bonnet chilli
2–4 dried chillies, seeded and torn
1 tbsp paprika
2 tsp ground cumin
¼ tsp ground cloves

¼ tsp ground cinnamon
250 ml (8 fl oz) vegetable stock
sea salt
1 400-g (14-oz) tin black beans
150 g (5 oz) frozen sweetcorn
1 tsp sugar
40 g (1½ oz) vegan dark chocolate
sliced avocados, lime juice, fresh coriander, to garnish

Preheat oven to 180°C (350°F/Gas mark 4). Process the pumpkin seeds or almonds in a food processor until very fine. Add the tomatoes and tahini and blend until smooth. Heat oil in a flameproof casserole, add the onion and cook for 5–7 minutes until soft. Add the garlic, pepper, plantain, squash, potatoes and fresh chilli. Cook for 3 minutes, then add the dried chilli and remaining spices. Cook for 1 minute. Add the tomato-tahini mixture and stock and season to taste. Bring to the boil, cover and cook in the oven 30 minutes. Remove from the oven and add the beans, sweetcorn and sugar, then stir in the chocolate until melted. Adjust seasoning and add a little water, if needed; the sauce should be thick and rich. Return to the oven for 10 minutes to heat through. Serve garnished with avocados dipped in lime juice and fresh coriander.
Serves 4

szechuan-glazed tofu with asparagus & cashew stirfry

see variations page 184

This upscale stirfry is sure to impress. Chilli garlic sauce is available in the Asian section of large supermarkets or in specialised food shops. If unavailable, use ketchup flavoured with garlic powder and Tabasco, to taste.

2 tbsp peanut or sunflower oil
2 cloves garlic, crushed
2.5-cm (1-inch) piece root ginger, grated
50 g (2 oz) sugar
125 ml (4 fl oz) water
2 tbsp chilli garlic sauce
1 tbsp cider vinegar
½ tsp red pepper flakes

500 g (1 lb 2 oz) extra-firm tofu (plain or smoked), pressed, drained and cut into triangles
1 bunch fresh asparagus, stalks peeled, diagonally sliced
½ red pepper, diagonally sliced very thinly

125 g (4 oz) baby spinach leaves
125 g (4 oz) toasted unsalted cashews
sea salt
chopped spring onions, to garnish
steamed rice, to serve

In a small pan, heat half the oil. Add the garlic and ginger and cook for 1 minute. Remove from the heat and add the sugar, water, chilli garlic sauce, vinegar and red pepper flakes. Return to the heat and bring to the boil, then reduce the heat and simmer for about 15 minutes until the sauce has a syrup-like consistency. Set aside and keep warm. Meanwhile, heat the remaining oil in a wok or heavy frying pan and cook the tofu until golden brown on all sides. Remove the tofu from the pan and keep warm. Stirfry the asparagus until tender-crisp, add the red pepper and stirfry for 1 minute. Add the spinach and stirfry until wilted. Return the tofu to the pan, add the cashews and mix. Pour the sweet and spicy sauce over the pan and serve on a bed of rice.

Serves 4

chestnut triangles with cranberry sauce

see variations page 185

This rich chestnut dish is a perfect winter warmer. Tinned chestnut purée is available in some supermarkets and food shops, but if unavailable, make your own by boiling shelled chestnuts in a little water and soya milk, then blending it to a thick paste.

1 tbsp sunflower oil
1 small onion, finely chopped
1 clove of garlic, crushed
125 g (4 oz) mushrooms, chopped
1 medium carrot, finely chopped
1 stalks celery, finely chopped
1 tbsp soya sauce

1 tbsp nutritional yeast
1/2 tsp dried thyme
1/4 tsp dried sage
1 tbsp chopped fresh parsley
125g (4 oz) unsweetened chestnut purée
4 tbsp vegetable stock (page 22) or half red wine, half stock

2 375-g (12-oz) blocks puff pastry, thawed if frozen
2 tbsp soya milk
black sesame seeds, to sprinkle
for the sauce
225 g (8 oz) brown sugar
125 ml (4 fl oz) orange juice
225 g (8 oz) fresh cranberries
$^{1}/_{2}$ tsp ground cinnamon

Heat 1 tablespoon oil in a flameproof casserole, add the onion and cook over medium-high heat for 5 to 7 minutes until it is soft. Add the garlic, mushrooms, carrots and celery. Cook for 5 minutes. Add the next seven ingredients, cook for 5 minutes, then allow to cool.

Roll each pastry block into a 32 cm (13 inch), square, trim and cut into 4 15-cm (6-inch) squares. Place the chestnut mixture in centre of each square. Brush the edges of squares with water, then fold in half to form triangles. Seal edges with a fork, then brush with soy milk and sprinkle with sesame seeds. Place on 2 baking trays. Cover and leave in the refrigerator for 1 hour or until required.

Meanwhile, make the sauce. Place the sugar and orange juice into a pan, bring to the boil, then stir in the cranberries and cinnamon. Cook for about 8 minutes until the cranberries are soft but are still holding their shape. Cover and keep chilled until required. Serve at room temperature.

Preheat oven to 200°C (400°F/Gas mark 6). Bake for about 20 minutes, until the pastry is puffed and golden brown. Serve with the cranberry sauce.

Makes 8 pastries

variations

refried bean tacos

see base recipe page 159

grilled vegetable & refried bean tacos
Prepare the basic recipe. Cut 2 small courgettes and 2 small yellow squash into 5-mm (¼-inch) thick slices, brush with sunflower oil and sprinkle with lime juice. Grill for 2 to 3 minutes on each side until cooked and browned. Add to the tacos with the beans.

refried bean & 'spicy sausage' tacos
Prepare the basic recipe, adding 300 g (10 oz) well-flavoured soya sausage, sliced, to the cooked onion. Fry, stirring frequently, for another 5 minutes before proceeding with the recipe.

refried bean & 'ground meat' tacos
Cook 350 g (12 oz) soya mince according to the package directions, then add to the basic recipe.

refried bean burritos
Prepare the basic recipe but spread the bean mixture in a warmed wheat tortilla, roll up and serve at once.

refried bean dip
Prepare the bean mixture and serve it cold with tortilla chips.

variations

three bean chilli

see base recipe page 160

three bean chilli with cheese & soured cream
Prepare the basic recipe and serve it garnished with grated vegan Cheddar-style cheese substitute and some non-dairy sour cream or soya yoghurt.

three bean chilli with tvp
Prepare the basic recipe. Ten minutes before the end of the cooking time, add 125 g (4 oz) dried TVP (texturised vegetable protein) that has been reconstituted in 125 ml (4 fl oz) water.

three bean enchiladas
Prepare half of the basic recipe. Warm 2 330-g (11-oz) tins enchilada sauce. Take 8 medium-size tortillas and dip each one in the sauce, fill with the chilli, roll up and place in a baking dish, then cover with the remaining sauce. Bake at 190°C (375°F/Gas mark 5) for 20 minutes.

three bean chilli potato bake
Prepare half of the basic recipe. Boil 500-g (1 lb 2 oz) potatoes, then mash with 25 g (1 oz) soya margarine and 4 tbsp soya milk; season with salt and pepper. Place the chilli in a baking dish and top with the mashed potatoes. Cook at 200°C (400°F/Gas mark 6) for 20 minutes or until golden.

variations

pasta e fagioli

see base recipe page 162

slow pasta e fagioli
Soak 200 g (7 oz) dried borlotti beans overnight, then drain. Prepare the basic recipe, adding the beans to the dish with the tomatoes. Cook for about 1½ hours, until the beans are tender.

pasta e lima fagioli
Prepare the basic recipe, using butter beans in place of the borlotti beans.

pasta e fagioli with smoked tofu
Prepare the basic recipe. Stir in 1 350-g (12-oz) package smoked tofu, crumbled, at the end of the cooking time.

pasta e fagioli soup
Prepare the basic recipe. Add about 500 ml (16 fl oz) extra stock with the pasta to make the dish more soupy.

variations

hippie hotpot

see base recipe page 163

green lentil hotpot
Prepare the basic recipe, using green lentils in place of the red lentils and cooking them for about 30 minutes.

curried lentil hotpot
Prepare the basic recipe, using 1 (10-ounce) jar curry sauce and 1 small chopped apple in place of the tomatoes, herbs and nutritional yeast.

lentil & sweet potato hotpot
Prepare the basic recipe, using 1 1/2 pounds sliced sweet potatoes in place of the potatoes.

lentil hotpot with 'cheesy' topping
Prepare the basic recipe, pouring 1 portion 'cheese' sauce (page 23) over the top of the potatoes before baking.

variations

lentil & quinoa burgers with mango salsa

see base recipe page 164

spicy lime, lentil & quinoa burgers with mango salsa
Prepare the basic recipe adding 1 or 2 finely chopped red chillies and the grated rind and juice of 1 lime to the mixture. If the mixture is too soft, add extra breadcrumbs.

lentil, quinoa & courgette burgers with mango salsa
Prepare the basic recipe, using 2 grated courgettes, squeezed of excess liquid in place of the carrot.

lentil & oat burgers with mango salsa
Prepare the basic recipe, omitting the quinoa. Add 90 g (3 oz) rolled oats with the breadcrumbs.

red lentil walnut burgers with mango salsa
Prepare the basic recipe, using 200 g (7 oz) red lentils, cooked and omitting the quinoa. Add 4 tablespoons each of rolled oats and finely chopped toasted walnuts with the breadcrumbs.

tomato farinata

see base recipe page 167

mushroom farinata

Prepare the farinata, omitting the topping. In its place, over medium heat cook 2 medium sliced mushrooms, 1 crushed clove of garlic and 1/2 teaspoon cumin in 2 tablespoons olive oil until the mushrooms are tender. Use to top the farinata.

lemon & courgette farinata

Prepare the farinata, but omit the topping. In its place, over a medium heat, cook 1 sliced small onion in 1 tablespoon olive oil until soft. Add 1 sliced medium courgette, 2 crushed cloves of garlic, 1 tablespoon chopped fresh parsley and the rind and juice of 1 small lemon. Cook until the courgette is tender, season with salt and pepper. Use to top the farinata.

herbed red onion farinata

Prepare the farinata, omitting the topping. In its place, over medium heat, cook 1 sliced large red onion in 1 tablespoon olive oil until soft. Add 2 sliced crushed cloves of garlic and 1 tablespoon each chopped fresh parsley and sage. Cook for 2 minutes, then season with salt and pepper. Use to top the farinata.

hungarian nut loaf

see base recipe page 168

moroccan nut loaf
Prepare the basic loaf recipe, using 2 or 3 teaspoons harissa in place of the paprika and caraway seeds, and fresh chopped coriander in place of the parsley and sage in the sauce.

indian spiced nut loaf
Prepare the basic recipe, using 1 or 2 tablespoons curry powder in place of the paprika and caraway seeds in the loaf. Add ½ teaspoon each of cumin and chilli powder to the sauce and use 1 tablespoon chopped fresh coriander in place of the sage.

provençal herbed nut loaf
Prepare the basic recipe, adding 12 sliced black olives and using herbes du Provence in place of the parsley and caraway seeds in the nut loaf. Use rosemary in place of the sage in the sauce.

mexican spiced nut loaf
Prepare the basic recipe, using 2 or 3 teaspoons hot chilli sauce in place of the paprika, cumin and caraway seeds in the nut loaf. Divide 1 220-g (4-oz) tin chopped green chillies between the nut loaf mixture and the sauce. Omit the pimento in the sauce and season it with hot chilli sauce, to taste.

variations

vegetable mole oaxaca

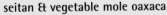

see base recipe page 171

seitan & vegetable mole oaxaca
Prepare the basic recipe. While the mole is cooking, fry 350 g (12 oz) chopped seitan in 1 tablespoon oil for 5 minutes, stirring frequently, then add to the mole with the sweetcorn.

tofu & vegetable mole oaxaca
Prepare the basic recipe. Take a 350-g (12-oz) block of tofu, which has been frozen and then thawed and cut it into chunks. Fry the tofu in 1 tablespoon oil until crispy. Add to the mole with the sweetcorn.

vegetable & mango mole oaxaca
Prepare the basic recipe, adding the chopped flesh of 1 mango with the sweetcorn.

vegetable mole bake
Prepare the basic recipe. Place a generous portion of the stew in a wheat tortilla, roll up and place in an oiled dish. Sprinkle with non-dairy cheese and bake for 20 to 25 minutes at 190°C (375°F/Gas mark 5) until crisp and golden. This is a good way to use leftover mole.

variations

szechuan-glazed tofu with asparagus & cashew stirfry

see base recipe page 172

szechuan-glazed tofu with bok choy, broccoli & water chestnut stirfry
Prepare the basic recipe, using 1 sliced head bok choy and 1 small head
broccoli, broken into florets, in place of the asparagus and sliced water
chestnuts in place of the cashews.

szechuan-glazed tofu with asparagus & walnut stirfry
Prepare the basic recipe, using toasted walnut pieces in place of
the cashews.

hoisin-glazed tofu with asparagus & cashew stirfry
Prepare the vegetables for the basic recipe. Replace the sauce with a sauce
made from mixing 6 tablespoons hoisin sauce and 1 tablespoon each of soya
sauce, rice wine (or dry sherry) and sesame oil plus 1 teaspoon grated fresh
root ginger.

szechuan black bean, asparagus & cashew stirfry
Prepare the basic recipe, replacing the tofu with 1 400-g (14-oz)
tin black beans, added after the spinach is just cooked and
heated through.

chestnut triangles with cranberry sauce

see base recipe page 174

chestnut triangles with mushroom-wine gravy
Prepare the chestnut triangles, but replace the cranberry sauce with gravy.
Cook a small onion and 4 ounces sliced mushrooms in 4 tablespoons oil until
just soft. Add 4 tablespoons flour, cook for 2 minutes, then slowly add 500
ml (16 fl oz) good vegetable stock, 150 ml (¼ pt) red wine, 2 tablespoons
soya sauce, 1 tablespoon nutritional yeast and ½ teaspoon each sage and
thyme. Cook gently, stirring constantly, until thickened; season with salt
and pepper.

smooth chestnut triangles with cranberry sauce
Prepare the basic recipe, but cooking the carrot and celery in stock until soft.
Purée in a blender before mixing with the chestnut purée and herbs.

black bean & mushroom triangles with cranberry sauce
Prepare the basic recipe, but purée a 400 g (14-oz) tin black beans and add
with the stock in place of the chestnut purée. Add 1 teaspoon Tabasco.

chestnut wellington with cranberry sauce
Prepare the basic recipe. Use 1 pre-rolled puff pastry sheet and place the
chestnut mixture in the centre, brush the edges with water and fold the
long sides together, pinch to seal, then seal together both ends. Continue as
for basic recipe cooking for about 40 minutes until golden.

rice, grain &
pasta dishes

In many cultures, vegans and non-vegans alike have

long appreciated the versatility of rice, grains and

pastas and their affinity with well-flavoured

vegetables. If any of these dishes are new to you,

give them a try and you'll soon be won over.

triple tomato risotto

see variations page 199

This very special risotto combines the rich intensity of roast cherry tomatoes and flecks of sun-dried tomato with the subtlety of tomato-flavoured bouillon.

350 g (12 oz) cherry tomatoes, halved
8 cloves of garlic
1 tbsp olive oil
1 l (1¾ pt) good vegetable stock
1 350-g (12-oz) jar tomato sauce
1 tbsp oil from sun-dried tomatoes
15 g (½ oz) soya margarine

4 shallots, finely chopped
400 g (14-oz) arborio (risotto) rice
125 ml (4 fl oz) white wine
40 g (1½ oz) sun-dried tomatoes, finely chopped
4 tablespoons chopped fresh basil
sea salt and black pepper

Preheat oven to 200°C (400°F/Gas mark 6). Put the cherry tomatoes and the unpeeled garlic in a single layer in an oiled baking dish and drizzle with the olive oil. Bake for about 30 minutes, until the tomatoes have shrivelled. Cool slightly, then squeeze the flesh out of the garlic, mash with a fork and set aside. In a small pan, heat the stock and tomato sauce until very hot; keep hot. Heat the tomato, oil and margarine in a saucepan, then add the shallots and cook for 5–7 minutes until soft. Add the rice and stir to coat it with oil, then cook until the grains become translucent, about 1 minute. Add the wine and cook, stirring until absorbed, then add about 1 ladleful of the hot stock mixture and continue to cook, stirring frequently, until fully absorbed. Add another ladleful of stock and allow it to be absorbed before adding another. Continue until rice is tender but firm and just coated in a thick sauce, about 20 minutes (you may not need all the stock). Gently stir in the cherry tomatoes, garlic, sun-dried tomatoes and basil and season with salt and pepper to taste. Serve immediately.

Serves 4

biryani

see variations page 200

Biryani was originally a dish created for the Moghul emperors and was a very complicated affair. This simple variation, which is very easy to cook, is packed with aromatic spices and makes a great party dish.

2 tbsp sunflower oil
1 large onion, finely sliced
3 cloves of garlic, crushed
2.5-cm (1-inch) piece root ginger, shredded
2 tsp black mustard seeds
1 red chilli pepper, finely sliced
3 tbsp madras curry paste
175 g (6 oz) each fresh cauliflower, carrot,
   green beans and potato, cut into chunks

175 g (6 oz) whole button mushrooms
1 l (1¾ pt) vegetable stock
175 g (6 oz) frozen peas
juice of 2 lemons
large pinch saffron threads
350 g (12 oz) basmati rice, washed
sea salt
2 tbsp chopped fresh coriander, to serve
150 g (5 oz) unsalted roasted cashew nuts or

Preheat the oven to 180°C (350°F/Gas mark 4). Heat the oil in a flameproof casserole, then add the onion and cook over medium-high heat for 5 to 7 minutes until the onion is soft. Add the garlic, root ginger, mustard seeds and chilli. Continue to cook, stirring, until the mustard seeds begin to pop. Stir in the curry paste, add the mixed vegetables and mushrooms, then stir well to coat. Pour in the stock and bring to the boil. Reduce the heat and simmer for 10 minutes, until the vegetables are nearly tender. Stir in the peas, lemon juice, saffron and rice, then season to taste with salt Cover with greaseproof paper, then with a tightly fitting lid and bake for 30 minutes, until the rice is tender and the stock is absorbed. To serve, sprinkle with coriander, cashews and raisins.

Serves 6–8

greek-style stuffed peppers

see variations page 201

To boost the protein level, add a tin of kidney beans or some diced firm tofu to the stuffing.

4 large green or red peppers
3 tbsp olive oil
1 medium onion, chopped
2 cloves of garlic, crushed
100 g (3½ oz) brown rice
600 ml (1 pt) tomato juice or vegetable juice
1 bay leaf
2 sprigs fresh parsley
2½ tsp dried oregano

100 g (3½ oz) chopped walnuts
1½ tbsp nutritional yeast
2 tsp lemon juice
pinch sugar
sea salt and black pepper
2 tbsp breadcrumbs
½ tsp lemon rind
1 tsp toasted sesame seeds

Cut the top off each pepper and remove the core and seeds. Brush the outside of the peppers with 1 tablespoon of the olive oil, then stand them upright in an ovenproof dish. Heat the remaining olive oil in a saucepan, then add the onion and cook 5–7 minutes until soft. Add the garlic and cook for another minute. Add the rice, half of the tomato juice, bay leaf, parsley and 2 teaspoons of the oregano. Bring to the boil, cover and simmer over low heat, adding extra water if the mixture dries out before the rice is cooked, about 40 minutes. Discard the bay leaf and parsley sprigs. Add the walnuts, 1 tablespoon nutritional yeast and lemon juice. Season with sugar, salt and pepper. Pile the mixture into the pepper shell. Preheat oven to 175°C (350°F/Gas mark 4). Pour remaining tomato juice and oregano around the peppers. Combine the breadcrumbs, remaining nutritional yeast, lemon rind and sesame seeds and sprinkle over the peppers. Bake 30–40 minutes until the peppers are tender. Serve hot.

Serves 4

caramelised onion polenta pie

see variations page 202

A great dish to cook ahead of time and it freezes well, too. Hot or cold, it is great accompanied by a salad, particularly one containing lots of ripe, juicy tomatoes.

1 red pepper, halved and seeded
1 yellow pepper, halved and seeded
1½ tbsp olive oil
25 g (1 oz) soya margarine
3 large onions, finely sliced
3 tbsp balsamic vinegar
1 tbsp brown sugar
2 bay leaves
sea salt and black pepper
2 tbsp chopped fresh parsley

1 tbsp chopped fresh thyme
175 g (6 oz) quick-cooking polenta
for the topping
75 ml (3 fl oz) tomato sauce
2 tbsp soya cream (optional)
2 tsp nutritional yeast
1 tsp paprika
pinch red chilli flakes
salt and black pepper
fresh parsley, to garnish

Put peppers under a hot grill and cook until the skin blackens. Turn and repeat until the whole peppers are charred. Wrap in clingfilm, allow to cool, then remove the skin and slice. Meanwhile, heat oil and margarine in a saucepan, add the onions and cook 5–7 minutes until soft. Reduce heat and stir in balsamic vinegar, brown sugar and bay leaves. Cook until onions are rich golden brown, about 20 minutes. Remove bay leaves and season to taste. Preheat oven to 200°C (400°F/Gas mark 6). Cook polenta according to package directions. While hot, stir in the peppers, onions, parsley and thyme. Check the seasoning. Oil a 23-cm (9-inch) round springform cake tin or a deep flan dish. Press the polenta mixture into the pan and leave to cool. Combine the ingredients for the topping, season to taste and spread over the top of the polenta. To serve, bake at 190°C (375°F/Gas mark 5) for 20 minutes until the top has browned.
Serves 6

millet pilaf with tahini-herb sauce

see variations page 203

Nutritionally, millet resembles wheat, providing niacin, vitamin B6 and folic acid along with some calcium, iron, potassium, magnesium and zinc. If you want fluffy, grainy millet, as for this dish, it is essential to leave it alone while cooking. If you want a soft textured millet, however, keep stirring until it is cooked.

4 tbsp olive oil
3 cloves of garlic
150 g (5 oz) millet
2 medium onions, thinly sliced
4 courgette, thinly sliced
2 green peppers, seeded and thinly sliced
75 g (3 oz) toasted pumpkin seeds
3 tbsp chopped fresh mint
rind and juice of 1 lemon

sea salt and black pepper
for the tahini-herb sauce
40 g (1½ oz) chopped fresh flat-leaf parsley
juice of 2 lemons
4 tbsp water
4 tbsp tahini
1 clove of garlic, crushed
agave nectar, to taste
sea salt and black pepper

Heat 2 tablespoons of the oil in a pan, add the garlic and millet and stir to coat all the grains in oil. Cover with plenty of boiling water and simmer for 20 minutes; drain. Meanwhile, heat the remaining oil in a separate pan and add the onions, courgette and peppers. Cover and cook over a low heat so the vegetables sweat in their own juices until just soft, stirring occasionally. Make the tahini-herb sauce by combining the ingredients by hand or in a food processor. Adjust the seasoning and sweetness to taste. Set aside. When the millet is cooked, stir in the cooked vegetables, pumpkin seeds, mint and lemon rind and juice. Season to taste with salt and pepper. Heat through, then serve with the tahini-herb sauce.

Serves 4

yakisoba

see variations page 204

The Japanese equivalent of junk food, this noodle dish is often sold at festivals and as street food, sometimes in a bun, hotdog style. It is quick to make, but to cut down the preparation time further, look out for bottled Yakisoba sauce in an Asian food market.

for the sauce
6 tablespoons teriyaki sauce
2 tbsp mirin (rice wine) or apple juice
2 tsp hot chilli sauce
1 lemongrass stalk, soft inner core only, crushed
    and finely sliced
1 tsp sugar
2 tsp sesame oil
for the stirfry
225 g (8 oz) soba noodles
1½ tbsp sunflower oil

1 small onion, sliced
2 cloves of garlic, grated
2 carrots, thinly sliced
½ head cabbage, shredded
4 spring onions, chopped
1 tbsp toasted sesame seeds
225 g (8 oz) firm tofu, pressed, drained and cut
    into 1-cm (½-inch) cubes
chopped spring onions or shredded seaweed, to
    garnish (optional)
pickled ginger, to garnish (optional)

Combine sauce ingredients in a small bowl and set aside. Cook the soba noodles in boiling water for about 2 minutes or until just cooked. Do not overcook or the noodles become sticky. Drain, rinse in cold water, then drain again. Heat the oil in a large frying pan or wok over medium-high heat. Add onions and stirfry for 2 minutes, then add garlic, carrots and cabbage. Stir-fry for 3–5 minutes, until vegetables are cooked but still firm. Add tofu, soba noodles, spring onions, sesame seeds and sauce, then cook, tossing to combine, until the noodles and tofu are hot. Serve garnished with chopped spring onions or seaweed and strips of pickled ginger, if desired.

Serves 4

sicilian caponata

see variations page 205

This heady dish captures the essence of the Sicilian summer. If strongly flavoured fresh tomatoes are available, use them; otherwise, the flavour of tinned plum tomatoes is preferable to hard, hothouse ones.

2 large aubergines
sea salt
2–3 tbsp olive oil
1 small red onion, finely chopped
2 stalks celery, chopped
2 cloves of garlic, crushed
1 tsp dried oregano
2 tbsp balsamic vinegar
2 tbsp salted capers

2 tbsp chopped fresh flat-leaf parsley
6 fresh tomatoes, skinned and chopped or 1
    400-g (14-oz) can chopped tomatoes
8 stoned green olives, halved
1 tsp sugar
black pepper
225 g (8 oz) spaghetti
olive oil, to toss

Cut the aubergine into 2.5-cm (1-inch) thick slices, then sprinkle with salt. Leave for 1 hour, then wipe away juices with kitchen paper. Cut into large chunks. Meanwhile, soak capers in water; drain. Heat 2 tablespoons olive oil in a frying pan and fry the aubergine chunks in batches over medium-high heat, stirring frequently until just golden all over but not cooked through. Add a little more oil, if required and do not overcook. Stir in onion, celery, garlic and oregano. Continue to cook about 5 minutes, until onion is soft and transparent. Pour in vinegar and cook, stirring, until it has evaporated. Add capers, parsley, tomatoes and olives. Season to taste with salt, pepper and sugar; cover and cook for 15–20 minutes, until the aubergine is tender. Meanwhile, cook the spaghetti following the package directions until al dente. Drain, toss with a little olive oil and serve immediately with the aubergine sauce.

Serves 4

creamy mushroom lasagne

see variations page 206

Supplement ordinary mushrooms with chestnut, chanterelle, Portobello, oyster, porcini or shiitake mushrooms to make this lasagne a taste sensation.

225 g (8 oz) lasagne noodles
100 g (3½ oz) dairy-free 'Parmesan' (page 22)
2 tbsp olive oil
1 large red onion, sliced
3 cloves of garlic, crushed
500 g (1 lb 2 oz) mixed fresh mushrooms, sliced
2 small leeks, white part only, chopped
2 tsp dried thyme

125 ml (4 fl oz) dry white wine
1 tbsp tamari
sea salt and black pepper
triple quantity of béchamel sauce (page 23)
3 tbsp nutritional yeast

For the pasta, cook lasagne according to package instructions. If using a no-cook variety, blanch in boiling water for 2 minutes. Drain and lay out on a tea towel or greaseproof paper. Meanwhile, heat the olive oil in a saucepan, then add the onion and cook over medium-high heat for 5 to 7 minutes until the onion is soft. Add the garlic, mushrooms, leeks and thyme and cook over low heat until the mushrooms are tender. Increase the heat, add the wine, allow to bubble for 2 minutes, then remove from the heat. Stir in the tamari and salt and pepper to taste. Make the béchamel sauce (page 23), then stir in the nutritional yeast. To assemble the lasagne, pour béchamel sauce over the bottom of a dish to form a thin layer, cover with a layer of pasta, coat with one-third of the béchamel sauce, followed by half the mushrooms, sprinkle with a third of the 'Parmesan'; repeat, finishing with a generous coating of 'Parmesan'. Preheat oven to 175°C (350°F/Gas mark 4). Cook for 30 minutes, then increase the heat to 200°C (400°F/Gas mark 6) and continue to cook until golden brown.

Serves 6–8

fusilli with french beans & tomatoes

see variations page 207

The rich tomato base used for this pasta dish is extremely versatile and can be adapted for many uses. If you haven't any red wine to hand, use 2 tablespoons of balsamic vinegar instead and make up the liquid with vegetable stock.

2 tbsp olive oil
3 cloves of garlic, crushed
1 medium onion, chopped
2 400-g (14-oz) tins chopped tomatoes
2 tbsp sun-dried tomato purée
125 ml (4 fl oz) vegetable stock
175 ml (6 fl oz) red wine

1 tbsp nutritional yeast
2 tsp dried Italian herbs
$^1/_2$ tsp sugar
sea salt and black pepper
450 g (1 lb) fusilli
olive oil, to coat
fresh basil, to garnish

Heat the oil in a frying pan, add the onion, then cook over medium-high heat for 5 to 7 minutes or until the onion is soft. Add the tomatoes, tomato purée, stock, wine, nutritional yeast, green beans, herbs and sugar. Season with salt and pepper. Bring to the boil, then cook for 20 to 25 minutes until the green beans are tender.

Cook the fusilli in boiling water for about 10 minutes or according to the package directions. The pasta should be cooked though but still firm. Drain, toss with olive oil and serve coated with the sauce and garnished with the basil.

Serves 4

variations

triple tomato risotto

see base recipe page 187

oven-baked triple tomato risotto
Prepare the basic recipe, using only 350 ml (12 fl oz) tomato sauce and 850 ml
(28 fl oz) stock. After the wine has been absorbed, add all the remaining
ingredients, cover and cook at 180°C (350°F/Gas mark 4) for 20 minutes; stir,
adding extra stock if required and continue to cook for 10 minutes or until the
rice is tender-firm.

triple tomato risotto cakes
Prepare the basic recipe, then let it cool. Shape the risotto into small cakes and
fry in olive oil until golden on both sides. This is an excellent way to use up
leftover risotto.

asparagus & tomato risotto
Prepare the basic recipe, using 1 bunch asparagus, chopped and blanched, in
place of the cherry tomatoes and garlic.

mushroom & tomato risotto
Prepare the basic recipe, using 100 g (3½ oz) cooked sliced button mushrooms,
in place of the roasted cherry tomatoes and garlic.

variations

biryani

see base recipe page 188

biryani with raita
Prepare the basic recipe and serve with raita. To 250 ml (8 fl oz) soya yoghurt, add 100 g (3¹/₂ oz) chopped cucumber, 1 chopped small red onion, 1 tablespoon chopped fresh mint and salt and lemon juice to taste.

lentil biryani
Prepare the basic recipe, adding 200 g (7 oz) rinsed brown lentils with the vegetables.

pumpkin biryani
Prepare the basic recipe, using a 350-g (12-oz) fresh pumpkin, cut into chunks, in place of the cauliflower and carrot.

biryani with fresh mango chutney
Prepare the basic recipe and serve with mango chutney (page 72).

variations

greek-style stuffed peppers

see base recipe page 190

stuffed courgette
Prepare the basic recipe, using 4 large courgettes, with seeds and some pulp scooped out, in place of the peppers.

barley-stuffed vegetables
Prepare the basic recipe, using barley in place of rice.

stuffed grape leaves
Prepare the basic recipe, using 1 225-g (8-oz) package of grape leaves in place of the peppers and 50 g (2 oz) pine kernels in place of the walnuts. Rinse the leaves in warm water, shake dry, lay out the leaves, vein-side up and roll 1 tablespoon of the mixture in each leaf. Place the parcels in a baking dish, cover with tomato juice mixture and weight the stuffed leaves with a plate to prevent unravelling. Omit the crumb topping. Serve cold.

persian stuffed peppers
Prepare the basic recipe, using 150 g (5 oz) cooked lentils (tinned or home-cooked) in place of the walnuts and 1 tablespoon each of fresh parsley and chives in place of the dried oregano. Add 65 g (2½ oz) currants to the rice mixture before cooking.

variations

caramelised onion polenta pie

see base recipe page 191

'cheesy' polenta pie
Prepare the basic recipe, using 175 g (6 oz) grated non-dairy 'cheese' in place of the onions.

roast vegetable polenta pie
Prepare the basic recipe, using the Mediterranean roasted vegetables (page 134) in place of the peppers, onions and herbs.

caramelised onions & tapenade polenta pie
Prepare the basic recipe, but cook without the topping. Spread tapenade (page 85) over the top of the hot pie and return to the oven for 2 minutes, just to heat through. Serve with a dollop of non-dairy sour cream or soya yoghurt.

mushroom polenta pie
Prepare the basic recipe, omitting the caramelised onions. Instead, cook 1 chopped onion in 2 tablespoons olive oil, add 1 crushed clove of garlic and 175 g (6 oz) sliced mushrooms. Cook gently until the mushrooms are tender. Add 1 tablespoon balsamic vinegar and cook until the liquid has evaporated. Stir into the polenta with the peppers and herbs.

millet pilaf with tahini–herb sauce

see base recipe page 193

barley pilaf
Prepare the basic recipe, using barley in place of millet. Dry toast the barley in a heavy-based pan for 3 to 4 minutes, stirring constantly, then cover with boiling water and simmer for 40 minutes until tender.

rice & almond pilaf
Prepare the basic recipe, using 200 g (7 oz) long-grain rice in place of the millet. After stirring the rice in the oil and garlic, cook the rice in a vegetable stock. Use toasted, slivered almonds in place of the pumpkin seeds.

wild rice pilaf
Prepare the basic recipe, using 200 g (7 oz) wild rice in place of the millet. After stirring the rice in the oil and garlic, cook the rice in 750 ml (24 fl oz) vegetable stock for about 50 minutes until the grains puff open. Drain and leave covered for 5 minutes.

buckwheat pilaf
Prepare the basic recipe, using 200 g (7 oz) buckwheat in place of the millet. After stirring the buckwheat in the oil and garlic, cover it with boiling water and cook for 5 minutes.

variations

yakisoba

see base recipe page 194

kata (crisp fried) yakisoba
Prepare the basic recipe. Once the noodles have boiled, drain thoroughly and pat dry. Alternatively purchase pre-steamed noodles. Heat oil in a deep- fat fryer or deep frying pan to 175°C (340°F). Divide noodles into 4 portions, then fry a portion at a time for 6 to 7 minutes, until they are crunchy. Serve the vegetables and sauce over the noodles.

yakisoba with yellow bean sauce
Prepare the basic recipe, omitting the sauce. Instead, combine 6 tablespoons teriyaki sauce; 4 tablespoons yellow bean sauce; 2 teaspoons grated root ginger; 1 lemongrass stalk, soft inner core only, crushed and finely chopped; and 2 teaspoons sesame oil.

yakisoba with 'chicken'
Prepare the basic recipe, using vegan soya-based 'chicken' in place of the tofu.

yakisoba bun
Prepare the basic recipe and serve in a hotdog bun garnished with vegan mayonnaise and pickled ginger.

variations

sicilian caponata

see base recipe page 195

spicy aubergine pasta
Prepare the basic recipe, adding ½–1 teaspoon harissa or Tabasco with
the onions.

sicilian-style squash pasta
Prepare the basic recipe, using 400 g (14 oz) diced winter squash or 3 large
courgette in place of the aubergine.

sicilian-style tomato & olive pasta
Prepare the basic recipe, omitting the aubergine. Sauté the onion, celery, garlic
and oregano in only 1 tablespoon olive oil. Add 2 additional large, fresh
tomatoes, skinned and chopped (or 1 225-g (8-oz) tin chopped tomatoes),
when making the sauce.

sicilian-style aubergine couscous
Prepare the basic recipe, using couscous in place of spaghetti. In a bowl, mix
300 ml (½ pt) boiling water and ½ teaspoon salt with 175 g (6 oz) quick-
cooking couscous. Cover and allow to stand for 5 minutes. Fluff with a fork.

variations

creamy mushroom lasagne

see base recipe page 196

vegan lasagne with 'cheese'
Prepare the basic recipe, adding 225 g (8 oz) grated non-dairy 'cheese' to the béchamel sauce (page 23).

creamy mushroom & fennel lasagne
Prepare the basic recipe, adding 2 sliced fennel bulbs, blanched for 5 minutes, with the mushrooms.

gluten-free mushroom spelt lasagne
Prepare the basic recipe, using spelt lasagne in place of the wheat-based lasagne noodles.

lasagne bolognese
Prepare the basic recipe, using bolognese sauce (page 207) in place of the mushroom filling.

fusilli with french beans & tomatoes

see base recipe page 198

fusilli arrabbiata
Prepare the basic recipe, omitting the French beans. Add to the tomato sauce, 1–2 teaspoons crushed red pepper flakes, 1 tablespoon lemon juice and 1 teaspoon paprika.

spaghetti bolognese
Prepare the basic recipe, using 225 g (8 oz) frozen vegan soya-based 'ground meat' in place of French beans.

spaghetti with pine nuts
Prepare the basic recipe, omitting the French beans. Add 50 g (2 oz) toasted pine kernels just before serving. Serve with spaghetti in place of fusilli.

fusilli with artichokes
Prepare the basic recipe, omitting the French beans. Add 1 250-g (12-oz) jar artichokes and a pinch of red pepper flakes 5 minutes before the end of the cooking time.

side dishes

Side dishes shouldn't be an afterthought. They are
as integral to the taste and appearance of the meal
as the main event. Think contrast – select fresh
bright flavours and intriguing textures – and think
artistically about the shape and colour of the meal
on the plate.

saffron rice

see variations page 221

Saffron is one of life's luxuries. It adds a lovely flavour to the rice and, with its little speckles of dense colour, looks fabulous too. If saffron is outside your budget, use 1 teaspoon of powdered turmeric instead.

800 ml (28 fl oz) vegetable stock
½ tsp saffron threads, soaked in 1 tbsp hot
  water
2 bay leaves
1 5-cm (2-inch) cinnamon stick

2 whole cloves
½ tsp sea salt
½ tsp dried chilli flakes (optional)
400 g (14 oz) Thai jasmine or white basmati
  rice

Place the stock, saffron and soaking water, bay leaves, cinnamon, cloves, salt and chilli flakes, if using, in a saucepan with a tight-fitting lid. Bring to the boil.

If using basmati rice, wash thoroughly to remove excess starch; jasmine rice does not need pre-washing. Add the rice to the pan, stir, cover and simmer over low heat for 10 to 15 minutes, until the rice is tender and the liquid is absorbed. Remove from the heat and, keeping the lid in place, let sit for 5 minutes. Discard the bay leaves and cinnamon stick, add the lemon juice, taste and adjust seasoning. Fluff with a fork before serving.

Serves 8

appams

see variations page 222

These spongy rice and coconut pancakes are much loved in the Christian communities in the southern Indian province of Kerela, where they are served with spicy curries and vegetable stews. However, they are also popular on their own with fresh chutneys or, for a breakfast treat, with coconut and sugar or syrup.

2 tbsp semolina
675 ml (22 fl oz) water
350 g (12 oz) rice flour
1 tsp sugar

1 tsp rapid-rise yeast
1 tsp sea salt
125 ml (4 fl oz) full-fat coconut milk

Place the semolina and 500 ml (16 fl oz) water in a pan over moderate heat. Bring to the boil, stirring continuously, then reduce the heat to low. Continue to cook and stir until a smooth paste is formed; transfer to a bowl and allow to cool. Add the rice flour, sugar and yeast. Stir in the coconut milk and remaining water to form a thick batter. Cover with clingfilm and let rise in a warm place for 3 to 4 hours, until the batter is bubbly and doubled in volume. Very carefully stir in the salt without beating the air out of the mixture.

Heat an oiled griddle or non-stick frying pan over a moderately high heat until very hot, add a ladleful of batter and spread it out by swirling the pan to form a thin pancake. Cover and cook for 3 to 4 minutes on one side only so that the base is lightly browned but the top remains very slightly moist; remove from the pan, keep warm and repeat with the remaining mixture.

Makes 10–12 pancakes

caramelised onion packets

see variations page 223

Cooking food in parchment seals in the flavour. Also, the food steams in its own juices, requiring less fat than pan-cooked vegetables. If you wish to adapt this recipe for the barbeque, use heavy-duty foil in place of parchment and cook the packet on a preheated grill for about the same time as the oven-cooked version.

24 baby onions or shallots, quartered
2 tbsp soya margarine
4 small sprigs fresh thyme
2 tbsp balsamic vinegar

2 tsp sugar
sea salt and black pepper
4 30-cm (12-inch) square pieces of
    parchment paper

Preheat oven to 200°C (400°F/Gas mark 6).

Melt the margarine in a pan and add the onions, shaking well to coat the onions evenly in margarine. Place one-quarter of the onions and a sprig of thyme in the centre of each of the paper squares, drizzle half a tablespoon balsamic vinegar over each, then sprinkle with sugar, salt and pepper.

Fold up the squares. It doesn't matter how you do this, but make sure that the seams are well rolled – the packets expand with steam during cooking so they need to be well sealed. Place on a baking tray in the oven and cook for 15 minutes, then shake the packets gently to move the contents about slightly and cook for another 30 minutes, until the onions feel soft if carefully squeezed through a cloth.

Serves 4

wholegrain mustard mash

see variations page 224

The ultimate comfort food is given a tangy twist with the addition of wholegrain mustard.

900 g (2lbs) floury potatoes, such as
   Maris Piper
2 cloves of garlic
250 ml (8 fl oz) soya milk
750 ml (1¼ pt) soya cream

1 bay leaf
sea salt
2 tbsp olive oil
1½ tbsp wholegrain mustard
black pepper

Peel the potatoes and cut each into 6 pieces. Peel and lightly crush the garlic. Place potatoes and garlic in a saucepan with the soya milk, cream, bay leaf and a generous pinch of salt. Cook for about 15 to 20 minutes, until the potatoes are very tender. Strain, reserving the cooking liquid but discarding the bay leaf and garlic.

Mash the potatoes thoroughly (do not use a blender or the potatoes may become gluey), then fold in enough cooking liquid for the mashed potatoes to become soft and smooth. Stir in the olive oil and the mustard, then season to taste with salt and pepper.

Serves 4–5

rösti

see variations page 225

The aroma of cooking rösti is irresistible! This Swiss potato pancake makes a great accompaniment for almost all dishes that do not contain potato. Rösti is also great on its own as a light lunch treat with a green salad or for breakfast served with grilled tomatoes or baked beans.

900 g (2 lb) potatoes, peeled
1 large onion, very finely chopped
2 tsp sea salt
½ tsp black pepper

4½ tbsp olive oil
3 tbsp chopped fresh chives
2 tbsp chopped fresh parsley

Bring a saucepan of water to a boil, add the potatoes and parboil for 4 minutes. Immediately remove the potatoes and place in cold water to cool. Once cool enough to handle, roughly grate them into a bowl. Add the onion, salt, pepper, 3 tablespoons of the oil, chives and parsley.

Heat the remaining oil in a non-stick frying pan over high heat. When it is very hot, add the potato mixture, pressing down firmly with the palm of your hand. Reduce the heat slightly, then cook until golden brown, about 7 minutes. Ease a spatula under the rösti to release, then invert the rösti onto a plate. Slip the rösti back into the pan to cook the second side. If preferred, the second side can be cooked under a preheated grill.

Serves 4

gingered pumpkin

see variations page 226

The sweetness of the pumpkin is accentuated in this recipe with the addition of maple syrup, which is cut with the sharpness of the ginger.

3 tbsp olive oil
1 500 g (1lb 2 oz) pumpkin, peeled and cut into
  2.5-cm (1-inch) chunks
1½ tsp grated root ginger

1 tsp caraway seeds
1 tbsp maple syrup
sea salt and black pepper

Heat the oil in a saucepan, then fry the pumpkin and ginger, turning often until the pumpkin is golden brown and crispy on the outside yet soft in the centre. Add the caraway seeds and maple syrup, then season with salt and pepper. Toss gently to coat and cook for another 2 minutes.

Serves 4

roast beetroot with satsuma–chipotle glaze

see variations page 227

Beetroot is a feast for the eyes as well as the taste buds. Here it is married with the sweet, tangy flavour of satsumas and balanced by the smoky taste of the pungent chipotle.

5 large fresh beetroot
125 ml (4 fl oz) fresh satsuma juice
1 tsp cornflour
1 tbsp cider vinegar
1½ tbsp agave nectar

1 tinned chipotle chilli, chopped, plus 1 tsp adobo sauce
2 tbsp soya margarine
strips of orange rind, to garnish
chopped fresh flat-leaf parsley, to garnish

Preheat oven to 190°C (375°F/Gas mark 5). Wash the beetroot, leaving the roots untrimmed. Place them on a large sheet of foil and seal into a package. Place the package in a roasting tin and roast for about 1¾ hours until the beetroot is tender; allow to cool. Once the beetroot are cool enough to handle, slip off the skins, then cut into 5-mm (¼-inch) slices.

Use 1 tablespoon of the satsuma juice to mix the cornflour to a paste. Add this paste, remaining satsuma juice, vinegar, agave nectar, chilli, adobo sauce and margarine to a saucepan. Cook gently until the sauce has slightly thickened. Add the beetroot slices and heat through, gently turning the beets to evenly coat with the glaze. Garnish with satsuma rind and chopped parsley.

Serves 6

creamed spinach

see variations page 228

Who said that you kiss goodbye to creamy tastes when you became a vegan? This delicious spinach dish is so quick and easy to make that it will earn its place on your list of favourites. You can make your own non-dairy cream cheese and mayo or purchase them from the health food shop. If you are in a hurry, you can leave out the onion and garlic.

1 tbsp olive oil
1 small onion, finely chopped
1 clove of garlic, crushed
500 g (1 lb 2 oz) fresh baby spinach, washed
125 g (4 oz) non-dairy cream cheese
50 g (2 oz) non-dairy mayonnaise

4 tbsp nutritional yeast
$\frac{1}{4}$ tsp ground nutmeg
$\frac{1}{4}$ tsp garlic granules
sea salt and black pepper
3 tbsp toasted slivered almonds, to garnish

Heat the olive oil in a saucepan, add the onion and cook over medium-high heat for 5 to 7 minutes until the onion is soft. Add the garlic and cook another minute. Add the spinach and cook with only the water clinging to the washed leaves until it is just tender; drain and transfer to a warmed serving dish.

Meanwhile, combine the non-dairy cream cheese, non-dairy mayonnaise, nutritional yeast, garlic granules and nutmeg in a saucepan. Heat gently without boiling, then season with salt and pepper to taste. Pour the sauce over the spinach, toss gently and garnish with the toasted almonds.

Serves 4

broccoli with tarator sauce

see variations page 229

Versions of tarator sauce are served all over the Middle East, sometimes as a dip, sometimes as a soup and sometimes, as here, to set off a vegetable or main dish. The common ingredient is always walnuts, although sometimes the sauce is flavoured with cucumber, tahini or even raisins. To make your tarator creamier, add a little soya yoghurt.

150 g (5 oz) whole walnuts
boiling water, to soak
1 large clove of garlic, crushed
75 g (3 oz) soft breadcrumbs
200 ml (7 fl oz) water
4 tbsp olive oil

2 tbsp lemon juice
1 tbsp white wine vinegar
pinch ground nutmeg
sea salt and black pepper
500 g (1 lb 2 oz) fresh broccoli, broken
    into florets

Soak the walnuts in boiling water for 1 hour. Drain and discard the water, then place the walnuts in a food processor with the garlic, breadcrumbs and about half of the water. Process until the texture suits your taste; the finer the grind, the smoother the finished sauce. Add the oil, lemon juice, vinegar and nutmeg and as much of the remaining water as necessary to make a thick but creamy sauce. Season to taste with salt and pepper. Leave for at least 2 hours to mature, then readjust the salt and vinegar if needed.

Stream the broccoli until tender-crisp. Serve immediately drizzled with some of the warm tarator sauce, serve the remaining sauce on the side.

Serves 4

variations

saffron rice

see base recipe page 209

lemon rice
Prepare the basic recipe, using 1 teaspoon powdered turmeric in place
of the saffron and adding the grated rind and juice of half a lemon. 50 g
(2 oz) cashews and/or 1 teaspoon mustard seeds (cooked for 1 minute in 1
teaspoon oil to pop) may also be added.

coconut rice
Prepare the basic recipe, using 75 g (3 oz) creamed coconut to the cooking
water in place of the spices.

rice with peas
Prepare the basic recipe, adding 150 g (5 oz) fresh or frozen cooked peas. This is
a good addition for the other variations, too.

vermicelli & rice
Prepare the basic recipe, omitting the saffron. Cook 75 g (3 oz) vermicelli broken
into 2.5-cm (1-inch) pieces in a frying pan with 2 tablespoons sunflower oil
until golden. Add to the boiling water with the rice.

variations

appams

see base recipe page 210

appams with onion & chilli
Prepare the basic recipe, adding a topping: cook 1 teaspoon black mustard seeds in 1 tablespoon oil until they pop. Add 1 finely chopped medium red onion, cook for 5 minutes. Add 1 sliced green chilli and 2 teaspoons cumin seeds and cook for 2 minutes. Stir in 4 tablespoons chopped fresh coriander and salt. Cook the appam for 3 minutes, top with a heaping tablespoon of the onion mixture, flip and cook the second side for 2 minutes.

sweet appams
Prepare the basic recipe, using only a pinch of salt. Just before cooking stir 4 tablespoons sugar into the batter. Cook for 3 to 5 minutes on one side only, until set. Serve with more agave or fruit syrup, shredded fresh coconut and fruit.

palappam (coconut appams)
Prepare the basic recipe, stirring in an additional 4 tablespoons coconut milk (plus 4 tablespoons agave nectar for sweet palappams) to the batter just before cooking. Cook for 3 to 5 minutes on one side only, until set.

variations

caramelised onion packets

see base recipe page 212

caramelised onion & potato packets
Prepare the basic recipe, with 12 baby onions and 12 small potatoes, scrubbed and quartered.

mushroom packets
Prepare basic recipe, but omit the sugar. Use 500 g (1 lb 2 oz) of mushrooms, quartered or sliced if large, in place of the onions. Bake for 15 to 20 minutes.

onion, pepper & peppadew packets
Prepare the basic recipe, but replace 12 of the onions with 1 red pepper, cut into 8 pieces; 4 quartered tomatoes; and 8 halved peppadew peppers from a jar. Omit the sugar.

caramelised red onion packets
Prepare the basic recipe, using 8 small red onions, quartered, in place of the baby onions or shallots.

variations

wholegrain mustard mash

see base recipe page 213

creamy mashed potatoes
Prepare the basic recipe, omitting the mustard.

pesto mashed potatoes
Prepare the basic recipe, using 2 tablespoons vegan pesto (page 74) in place of the mustard.

potato & celeriac mash
Prepare the basic recipe, using 500 g (1 lb 2 oz) each of potatoes and celeriac and 1 teaspoon Dijon mustard in place of the wholegrain mustard.

roast garlic mashed potatoes
Prepare the basic recipe, using the flesh from 6 roast garlic cloves with the potatoes.

variations

rösti

see base recipe page 215

rösti with onion & caraway
Prepare the basic recipe, adding 1 tablespoon toasted caraway seeds with
the herbs.

rösti with nondairy cheese
Prepare the basic recipe. Add 175 g (6 oz) grated non-dairy hard cheese to the
grated potato mixture.

rösti with leftover vegetables
Prepare the basic recipe. Add 125 g (4 oz) leftover cooked vegetables, chopped
into small pieces, to the shredded potato mixture.

rösti pizza
Prepare the basic recipe and just lightly cook the rösti on one side. Spread pizza
sauce over that lightly cooked side and top with slices of mushroom, pepper and
onion. If desired, sprinkle with non-dairy 'Parmesan' cheese. Place under a
preheated grill until the vegetables are cooked.

variations

gingered pumpkin

see base recipe page 216

gingered pumpkin with red chilli oil
Before cooking the pumpkin and ginger, heat the olive oil over a
low heat with 1 sliced, large red chilli; 2 whole unpeeled garlic cloves; ¼
teaspoon cumin seeds; and 1 strip of lemon rind. Cook until the garlic is
browned, then strain and proceed as in the basic recipe.

gingered plantain
Prepare the basic recipe, using plantain in place of pumpkin.

gingered swede
Replace the pumpkin with 500 g (1 lb 2 oz) roughly chopped swede,
parboiled for 5 minutes in boiling water and drained. Add this to the oil with
the ginger and continue as in the basic recipe.

gingered sweet potato
Replace the pumpkin with 500 g (1 lb 2 oz) chopped sweet potato, parboiled
for 5 minutes in boiling water and drained. Add this to the oil with the
ginger and continue as in the basic recipe.

variations

roast beetroot with satsuma chipotle glaze

see base recipe page 217

rosemary & orange roast beetroot
Prepare the basic recipe, adding 2 sprigs fresh rosemary to the foil packages.
Stir 1 teaspoon chopped fresh rosemary into the glaze in place of the chipotle
and adobo sauce.

broccoli with satsuma chipotle glaze
Prepare the chipotle glaze. Steam 1 head of broccoli, cut into florets, until
tender-crisp. Glaze as with the beetroot.

chipotle roast carrot & parsnip
Prepare the basic recipe, roasting 3 parsnips and 3 carrots in place of the
beetroot. Peel and chop the vegetables into 4 pieces, put in an aluminium foil
package, drizzle with 1 teaspoon olive oil and roast for about 1 hour until
tender. Slip the carrots and parsnips into the glaze directly from the package.

sweet potato & red onion with satsuma chipotle glaze
Prepare the basic recipe, roasting 750 g (1½ lb) sweet potatoes and 2 red
onions in place of the beets. Peel and chop the vegetables into 4 to 6 pieces
and continue as in the chipotle variation above.

variations

creamed spinach

see base recipe page 218

creamed kale
Prepare the basic recipe, using 500 g (1 lb 2 oz) kale in place of
the spinach.

pasta with creamed spinach
Prepare the basic recipe and serve it over 340 g (12 oz) cooked pasta such as
gnocchi or fusilli.

creamed spinach & leeks
Prepare the basic recipe, adding 3 sliced leeks (white part only) to the pan with
the onion. Use just 250 g (9 oz) spinach.

cauliflower 'cheese'
Prepare the basic recipe, replacing the spinach with 1 cauliflower, broken into
florets and cooked in boiling water until tender. For a more cheesy flavour, add
175 g (6 oz) shredded non-dairy, Cheddar-style 'cheese' to the sauce.

variations

broccoli with tarator sauce

see base recipe page 220

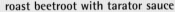

roast beetroot with tarator sauce
Prepare the sauce for the basic recipe. Roast the beetroot (page 217). Spoon the tarator over the hot beetroot. Also use the beetroot greens, if you wish; steam them for 5 minutes or until wilted and just tender.

french beans with tarator sauce
Prepare the basic recipe, using 500 g (1 lb 2 oz) French beans in place of the broccoli.

cucumber salad with tarator sauce
Omit the broccoli. Prepare the basic sauce. Make a salad of sliced cucumber sprinkled with a little salt and tossed with 1 tablespoon chopped fresh dill. Lay salad on a bed of watercress and serve with the chilled tarator sauce.

bulgarian tarator soup
Omit the broccoli. Prepare the basic sauce, omitting the vinegar. Stir in 1 l (1¾ pt) soya yoghurt and 1 finely chopped, peeled cucumber and 1 tablespoon chopped fresh dill. Chill thoroughly before serving.

desserts

There is nothing better than rounding off a meal with a yummy dessert. This selection contains something delectable for everyone - for chocolate lovers, pie or ice cream lovers and for those who like their desserts rich and creamy.

silken chocolate mousse

see variations page 246

This recipe is almost too easy to be true, and non-vegans will be truly astonished when they try this amazing mousse. It is very rich, so serve it in small bowls.

1 350-g (12-oz) package silken tofu, room
    temperature, drained
275 g (10 oz) plain vegan chocolate
3 tbsp maple syrup

1 tsp vanilla essence
2 tbsp amaretto or a few drops almond essence
fresh raspberries and mint leaves, to garnish

Beat the tofu by hand or in a food processor until smooth.

In a double boiler, melt the chocolate, stirring frequently, until smooth. Add to the tofu with the maple syrup, vanilla and amaretto or almond essence and beat by hand to combine. Pour into small dishes and chill for at least 30 minutes. Serve garnished with raspberries and mint leaves.

Makes 4 large or 6 small servings

pistachio kulfi

see variations page 247

Kulfi is Indian ice cream flavoured with pistachio, rosewater or mango. This version uses coconut and soya milk to replace the traditional slow-cooked sweet milk. It is delicious and lighter than the original. Kulfi moulds are conical in shape and can be purchased at some Asian stores; however, silicone muffin pans work really well too.

75 g (3 oz) shelled pistachios
1 tbsp ground almonds
500 ml (16 fl oz) soya or almond milk
250 ml (8 fl oz) full-fat coconut milk
50 g (2 oz) icing sugar

$1/2$ tsp crushed cardamom seeds
1 tsp vanilla essence
few drops almond essence
fresh mango slices or passion fruit pulp, to
serve

Place the pistachios in a blender and process until chopped. Remove about three-quarters of the pistachios and set aside. Process the remaining pistachios until ground, then add the ground almonds and about one-quarter of the soya or almond milk. Mix in the remaining ingredients by hand, including the chopped pistachios. If the coconut milk remains a bit lumpy, this is good because it adds to the texture of the kulfi. Pour the mixture into an ice cream maker and process until the ice cream has set. Transfer it into the moulds. Alternatively, place mixture in a freezer container and freeze for about 4 hours, removing from the freezer every hour and mashing with a fork to break down the ice crystals. Transfer into moulds to finish freezing. Remove from the fridge 10 minutes before serving. Serve with slices of mango or drizzle it with passion fruit pulp.

Makes 6

apple strudel

see variations page 248

Using filo pastry, this dessert is quick to construct and very impressive when it comes out of the oven. See page 15 for hints on working with filo dough.

rind and juice of ½ lemon
4 medium cooking apples
50 g (2 oz) finely chopped pecans
25 g (1 oz) soft, fresh breadcrumbs
2 tsp ground cinnamon

175 g (6 oz) brown sugar
4–6 sheets filo pastry 30x44 cm (11x17-inch))
4 tbsp rapeseed or safflower oil
50 g (2 oz) sultanas
icing sugar, to finish

Preheat the oven to 180°C (350°F/Gas mark 4). Fill a bowl with cold water and add the lemon juice. Peel and slice the apples, putting them into the water to prevent them from browning. In a separate bowl, combine the pecans, breadcrumbs, cinnamon and half of the brown sugar. Place the first sheet of filo pastry on a clean tea towel on your work surface and brush with oil. Sprinkle with a third of the pecan mixture. Place another sheet of filo pastry on top, brush with oil and sprinkle with another third of the pecan mixture; repeat with the third sheet, then lay the fourth sheet on top. Drain the apples and pat dry, then mix them with the remaining sugar, lemon rind and sultanas. Lay the apples evenly along the length of the filo but no more than halfway across it and leaving a 2-cm (¾-inch) margin around the edges. Brush the edges with a little water. Roll up the dough lengthwise, using the cloth to help support the dough; press the strudel together gently. Place the strudel on a silicone sheet or on greaseproof paper on a baking tray and bake for about 20 minutes or until golden brown. Serve hot or at room temperature, sprinkled with icing sugar and with a scoop of non-dairy ice cream (page 239).

Serves 6–8

baked rice pudding

see variations page 249

Comfort food at its best. This version is healthier and lower in fat than the traditional dessert, so it is good for you too. It cooks very slowly in a low oven, so you can bake it while you get on with other things.

5 tbsp short-grain rice
3 tbsp brown sugar or 2 tbsp agave nectar
1 strip lemon rind or 1 vanilla pod
1.1 l (2 pt) soya or other unsweetened
   non-dairy milk

¼ tsp grated nutmeg
2 tbsp non-dairy margarine or buttery spread

Preheat oven to 150°C (300°F/Gas mark 2).

Generously grease a 1.1-l (2-pint) ovenproof dish with margarine or buttery spread. Place the rice, brown sugar or syrup and lemon rind or vanilla pod in the dish. Gently pour in the milk and stir. Sprinkle the grated nutmeg over the surface of the milk and dot with margarine or buttery spread.

Carefully transfer to the oven and bake for 45 minutes, stir, then let it cook for another 75 minutes, by which time a brown crust will have formed and the rice will be fully cooked. Serve hot.

Serves 4

tropical fruit kebabs

see variations page 250

We don't often think about using the barbecue to cook dessert, but these kebabs make a tasty end to an outdoor meal. If you prepare the kebabs in advance, brush the banana and mango with a little lemon juice to prevent browning, cover with clingfilm and keep cool. The syrup can be reheated when required.

for the syrup
75 g (3 oz) non-dairy margarine or spread
6 tbsp maple syrup
6 cardamom pods, seeds only
1 whole clove
1 7.5-cm (3-inch) cinnamon stick
$\frac{1}{2}$ tsp vanilla essence

for the kebabs
$\frac{1}{2}$ small pineapple
2 ripe mangoes
2 firm bananas
nondairy ice cream (page 239), to serve

In a small pan, melt the non-dairy margarine and stir in the maple syrup. Crush the cardamom seeds with a mortar and pestle, then add them to the syrup with the clove, cinnamon and vanilla. Keep warm to infuse while preparing the fruit. Skin and core the pineapple and cut into 2.5-cm (1-inch) chunks. Cut the mango flesh into large chunks, then remove the skin. Peel the bananas and cut into 2.5-cm (1-inch) slices. Thread fruit onto 8 metal skewers or wooden skewers that have been soaked in water for 30 minutes to prevent burning. Preheat barbecue or grill to medium-hot. Remove the clove and cinnamon stick from the syrup. Place the kebabs on an oiled rack and cook, turning once and basting frequently with the syrup until fruit is lightly browned on the outside, about 5 minutes. Do not overcook or the fruit will fall apart. Drizzle with any remaining syrup and serve immediately with non-dairy ice cream.
Serves 4

chocolate chip soya ice cream with hot chocolate sauce

see variations page 251

A low-fat indulgence and it's versatile too. For vanilla flavour, simply omit the chocolate.

2 tbsp arrowroot
250 ml (8 fl oz) soya milk
500 ml (16 fl oz) soya cream
4 tablespoons agave nectar or 75 g (3 oz) sugar
pinch salt
2 tsp vanilla essence

175 g (6 oz) small chunks plain vegan chocolate
for the chocolate sauce
50 g (2 oz) non-dairy margarine
175 g (6 oz) brown sugar
50 g (2 oz) plain vegan chocolate, chopped
3–4 tbsp soya milk

Mix the arrowroot to a paste with 2 tablespoons of the soya milk; set aside. In a saucepan, combine the remaining milk, non-dairy cream, syrup or sugar and salt and bring to the boil. While stirring, pour the arrowroot paste into the pan, stirring until the mixture thickens slightly. The mixture will continue to thicken as it cools. Taste and adjust sweetening. Cover the surface with greaseproof paper or clingfilm to prevent a skin from forming. When the mixture is cool, stir in the vanilla essence and the chocolate chips. Pour the mixture into an ice cream maker and process until the ice cream has set. Alternatively, place it in a freezer container and freeze for about 6 hours. Remove from the freezer every 1½ hours and mash with a fork to break down the ice crystals to form a smooth ice cream. To make the sauce, melt the non-dairy margarine in a pan, add the sugar and cook, stirring, over low heat until melted. Add the chocolate and 3 tablespoons soya milk, stir until melted and add a little more soya milk, if desired. Serve hot over the ice cream.

Makes 1 litre (1³/₄ pints)

caramelised apple crisp

see variations page 252

During the autumn when the choice of apples at the farmers' market is abundant, this dish comes into its own. Blenheim Orange, Crispin and Egremont Russet are all delicious and of course, Granny Smith apples are available year-round.

50 g (2 oz) soya margarine
175 g (6 oz) brown sugar
5 tart apples, peeled and sliced
75 g (3 oz) whole wheat pastry flour
50 g (2 oz) oat-based muesli

1 tsp ground cinnamon
$\frac{1}{2}$ tsp ground nutmeg
4 tbsp rapeseed or sunflower oil
2 tbsp almond or soya milk

Preheat oven to 200°C (400°F/Gas mark 6). In a frying pan, melt the margarine, then add two-thirds of the brown sugar. Cook, stirring constantly, until the sugar has melted. Add the apples and turn to coat in the caramel mixture, then cook for about 10 minutes, stirring frequently, until the apples are cooked but still firm.

Meanwhile, in a bowl, combine the remaining brown sugar with the rest of the ingredients, mixing lightly with the fingertips until the mixture becomes crumbly. Add a little more oil if the mixture is too dry or a little more flour if it is too sticky.

Transfer the apples to a deep pie dish or casserole dish and top with the crumb mixture. Bake for 30 minutes or until crisp and golden. Serve with soya vanilla 'ice cream' (page 239).

Serves 6

toffeed bananas with coconut cream

see variations page 253

Rich but light, this coconut cream is a wonderful accompaniment to most fruit-based desserts.

for the coconut cream
125 g (4 oz) block creamed coconut
75 ml (3 fl oz) coconut, almond milk
4 tbsp soya yoghurt

4 firm, ripe bananas
1 tbsp lemon juice
2 tbsp brown sugar
pinch ground cinnamon
pinch ground nutmeg
toasted coconut, to garnish

To make the coconut cream, roughly chop the block of creamed coconut into pieces and place them in a saucepan with the coconut, almond or soya milk. Heat slowly until the coconut has melted, stirring frequently. Remove and allow to cool. Add the yoghurt to the cooled coconut cream, beating until the mixture resembles whipped cream in texture. Allow to cool and keep refrigerated until required.

Peel the bananas, cut them in half lengthwise, brush with lemon juice and place in a shallow pan. Sprinkle them with the brown sugar and a pinch of cinnamon and nutmeg. Place under a medium-hot grill under the sugar is beginning to caramelise and the bananas are soft. Do not overcook. Serve hot with the coconut cream and garnish with toasted coconut.

Serves 4

no cheesecake with mixed berries

see variations page 254

This creamy dessert is stunning – all the joy of cheesecake with a fraction of the fat.

50 g (2 oz) soya margarine
225 g (8 oz) vegan digestive biscuits, crushed
1 tbsp cornflour
3 tbsp soya milk
1 350-g (12-oz) package silken tofu, drained
225 g (8 oz) non-dairy cream cheese
175 ml (6 fl oz) soya yoghurt

juice and rind of ½ lemon
egg replacer for 1 egg (page 24)
1 tbsp water
25 g (1 oz) icing sugar, sifted
½ tsp vanilla essence
225 g (8 oz) fresh mixed berries
2 tbsp redcurrant jelly, melted

Preheat oven to 180°C (350°F/Gas mark 4). Oil an 20-cm (8-inch) cake tin with a removable base. In a saucepan, melt the margarine. Combine 2 tablespoons of the melted margarine with the crushed digestive biscuits, then press into the cake tin. Bake for 10 minutes, then set aside. Meanwhile, to the remaining melted margarine in the saucepan, stir in the cornflour, then blend in the soya milk. Cook over low heat until thickened. In a bowl or blender, beat the tofu, non-dairy cream cheese, yoghurt and lemon juice and rind until smooth. In a cup, whisk the egg replacer with the water until frothy (or as directed on the package) and stir into the tofu mixture. Mix in the cornflour mixture, icing sugar and vanilla. Pour the mixture over the prepared base and cook for 30 minutes or until the edge of the cheesecake just begins to colour. The centre will still feel wobbly, but it will firm up when cool. When the cheesecake is cool, arrange the berries on top and lightly brush them with the melted redcurrant jelly to glaze. Place cheesecake in the fridge to chill. Serve it straight from the fridge.

Serves 8–10

strawberry tart

see variations page 255

Simple and easy to prepare, a seasonal fruit tart looks and tastes wonderful. Leftover pastry can be made into jam tarts, which are surprisingly popular with young-at-heart adults and children alike.

1 recipe wholemeal pastry
500 g (1 lb 2 oz) ripe strawberries, halved
small fresh mint leaves
for the glaze
125 g (4 oz) granulated sugar

4 tbsp cornflour
250 ml (8 fl oz) water
4 tbsp strawberry jam
1 tbsp lemon juice

Preheat oven to 200°C (400°F/Gas mark 6). Lightly butter a 23-cm (9-inch) flan tin. Roll out the pastry on a floured surface, use it to line the flan tin and chill for 20 minutes. Line the base of the pastry with greaseproof paper weighed down with baking beans, then bake for 12 minutes. Reduce the heat to 140°C (275°F/Gas mark 1) and bake for 10 minutes more. Remove the parchment and beans and cook for another 10 minutes for the pastry to dry out. Cool.

To make the glaze, mix together all the ingredients in a saucepan. Bring to the boil and cook, stirring for 1 minute, until thickened. Remove from heat and cool slightly.

Spread half of the warm glaze over the cooked crust. Top with the strawberries, then brush the remaining warm glaze over the strawberries. Allow to cool and serve cold, garnished with small mint leaves.

Serves 6–8

variations

silken chocolate mousse

see base recipe page 231

chocolate mousse french-style
Prepare the basic recipe, using 2 tablespoons cognac in place of
the amaretto.

chocolate orange mousse
Prepare the basic recipe, using 3 tablespoons Grand Marnier, triple sec or
orange juice in place of the amaretto and vanilla.

chocolate mousse dip with pineapple and strawberries
Prepare the basic recipe. Serve it warm as a dip for chunks of pineapple and
whole strawberries.

peanut butter chocolate mousse pie
Prepare the basic recipe. Take one small prepared pastry case, spread it with
a thin layer of peanut butter and top it with the chocolate mousse.

chocolate truffles
Prepare the basic recipe, using 225 g (8 oz) sifted icing sugar in place of
maple syrup. Chill the mixture for 2 hours, then, working quickly, roll the
mixture into small balls. Roll them in cocoa powder, icing sugar or shredded
coconut. Drop truffles into paper sweet cases to serve.

variations

pistachio kulfi

see base recipe page 232

pistachio rosewater kulfi
Prepare the basic recipe, adding 2 tablespoons rosewater to the ingredients. Serve sprinkled with a few drops of rosewater and garnished with edible rose petals.

mango kulfi
Prepare the basic recipe, using only 1 tablespoon pistachios, ground to a powder and adding the finely chopped flesh from 1 ripe mango to the mixture.

saffron almond kulfi
Prepare the basic recipe, using 225 g (8 oz) blanched almonds in place of the pistachios. Add a pinch of saffron to the mixture and serve garnished with chopped pistachios.

malai kulfi
Prepare the basic recipe, omitting the pistachios.

variations

apple strudel

see base recipe page 234

apple & cranberry strudel
Prepare the basic recipe, using dried cranberries in place of the golden raisins.

apple & pear strudel
Prepare the basic recipe, using 2 apples and 2 pears.

apple & plum strudel
Prepare the basic recipe, using 2 apples and 4 roughly chopped, medium-sized plums. (The plum pieces do not need to wait in the acidulated water.)

peach & cardamom strudel
Prepare the basic recipe, using 4 large, peeled and stoned, ripe peaches in place of the apples (the peach slices do not need to wait in the acidulated water). Omit the sultanas and use 1 teaspoon ground cardamom in place of the cinnamon.

baked rice pudding

see base recipe page 235

caribbean coconut rice pudding
Prepare the basic recipe, using 375 ml (12 fl oz) coconut milk and 625 ml (1 pt) soya milk. Add 2 tablespoons raisins and 2 tablespoons flaked coconut with the rice.

chocolate rice pudding
Prepare the basic recipe, using chocolate soya milk in place of the unsweetened soya milk. Use a little of this milk to mix with 2 tablespoons cocoa powder to form a paste, then add it to the rice.

egyptian rice pudding
Prepare the basic recipe, using lemon rind option. To the rice, add 2 lightly crushed cardamom pods, a pinch of saffron and 2 tablespoons rosewater.

caramel rice pudding
Combine 3 tablespoons sugar and 3 tablespoons water in a small pan and cook gently, stirring, until dissolved; increase the heat slightly and continue to cook, without stirring, until a golden caramel is formed. Do not overcook; brown caramel is bitter. Immediately stir in 250 ml (8 fl oz) of the soya milk (be careful, as it will splatter), pour mixture into the prepared dish and continue as with the basic recipe.

variations

tropical fruit kebabs

see base recipe page 236

orchard fruit kebabs
Prepare the basic recipe, replacing the tropical fruit with 1 large apple and
1 large pear, chopped into 2.5-cm (1-inch) chunks and coated with lemon
juice and 6 halved plums.

tropical fruit & bagel kebabs
Prepare the basic recipe. Cut a bagel in half and spread with nondairy
butter, then sprinkle with brown sugar and cinnamon. Cut each bagel half
into 6 pieces and thread them on the skewers with the fruit.

tropical fruit kebabs with orange cinnamon syrup
Prepare the basic recipe, adding 2 tablespoons orange juice concentrate in
place of the vanilla in the syrup.

tropical fruit kebabs with chocolate sauce
Prepare the basic kebabs and serve with chocolate sauce (page 239).

variations

chocolate chip soya ice cream with hot chocolate sauce

see base recipe page 239

double chocolate chip soya ice cream with hot chocolate sauce
Prepare the basic recipe. Mix 4 tablespoons cocoa powder to a paste with a little of the soya milk and add to the pan with the remaining soya milk. Alternatively, use chocolate-flavoured soya milk. When cool, add 175 g (6 oz) chopped vegan white, milk or plain chocolate.

peppermint chocolate chip soya ice cream with hot chocolate sauce
Prepare the basic recipe for double chocolate chip soya ice cream (above), using 1 tablespoon peppermint essence in place of the vanilla.

strawberry soya ice cream
Prepare the basic recipe, adding 225 g (8 oz) crushed strawberries with the vanilla. The same principle applies for other berries and for mango or peach ice cream. Serve alone or if desired, with the chocolate sauce.

banana 'milkshake'
Prepare the basic recipe, omitting the sauce. Place in a blender 250 ml (8 fl oz) ice-cold soya or coconut milk, 4 scoops of vanilla soya ice cream (see variation above), 1 thickly sliced banana and ½ teaspoon vanilla essence; blend until smooth.

variations

caramelised apple crisp

see base recipe page 240

caramelised peach crisp
Prepare the basic recipe, using 5 medium, ripe peaches in place of the apples. Add 1 tablespoon rum with the peaches for extra flavour.

caramelised apple ginger crisp
Prepare the basic recipe, adding 3 tablespoons chopped crystallised ginger to the apple mixture.

caramelised apple scone bake
Prepare the apples for the basic recipe. Make scones (page 133), using 1 tablespoon sugar in place of the rosemary. Arrange the scones on top of the apples and bake as directed.

caramelised apple crêpe
Prepare the apples for the basic recipe. Make a batch of crepes (page 126). Stuff the crepes with the apples, arrange in an greased baking dish and bake at 220°C (425°/Gas mark 7) for 20 minutes or until golden.

variations

toffeed banana with coconut cream

see base recipe page 241

toffeed pineapple with coconut cream
Prepare the basic recipe, using 8 slices fresh or tinned pineapple in place of the bananas. Omit the lemon juice.

toffeed nectarines with coconut cream
Prepare the basic recipe, using 4 large, ripe nectarines, skinned, stoned and halved, in place of the bananas.

red fruit salad with coconut cream
Prepare the coconut cream. To make the salad, combine 350 g (12 oz) cubed watermelon, 225 g (8 oz) strawberries, 125 g (4 oz) raspberries, the seeds from 1 pomegranate and 2 chopped plums. Sprinkle with 1 or 2 tablespoons sugar and 4 tablespoons cranberry juice and serve with the coconut cream.

asian fruit salad with coconut cream
Prepare the coconut cream. To make the salad: In a saucepan, dissolve 125 g (4 oz) sugar in 500 ml (16 fl oz) water, bring to the boil, then add 1 star anise, 1 strip orange rind and 1 split vanilla pod. Simmer until reduced by half; cool. Strain and pour over a salad made from half a pineapple, 12 lychees, 1 papaya, 1 star fruit and the pulp from a passion fruit.

variations

no cheesecake with mixed berries

see base recipe page 242

pumpkin no cheesecake with maple syrup pecans
Prepare the basic recipe, adding 275 g (10 oz) pumpkin purée to the tofu mixture. Replace the vanilla with 1 teaspoon ground cinnamon. For the topping, instead of the berries, toss 150 g (5 oz) whole pecans with 3 tablespoons maple syrup, 1 tablespoon sugar and ¼ teaspoon cinnamon. Bake topping on baking sheet at 180°C (350°F/Gas mark 4) for 10 minutes; cool before using to decorate cheesecake.

no cheesecake with ginger & pineapple
Prepare the basic recipe, omitting topping. Add 1 teaspoon ground ginger to the graham cracker crumbs. Top the cheesecake with slices of fresh or canned pineapple and chopped crystallised ginger.

raspberry no cheesecake
Prepare the basic recipe, adding 125 g (4 oz) raspberries to the mixture with the vanilla. Use 175 g (6 oz) raspberries in place of the mixed berries for the topping.

chocolate no cheesecake
Prepare the basic recipe, replacing the digestive biscuits with Oreo cookies. To the filling, stir in 175 g (6 oz) vegan chocolate, melted, in place of the lemon juice and rind and add 10 broken Oreo cookies.

variations

strawberry tart

see base recipe page 245

strawberry & cream tart
Prepare the basic recipe, halving the ingredients for the strawberry preserve
glaze. Prepare one portion of nondairy whipped cream (page 21). Spread a very
thin layer of glaze over the base of the tart to seal, then cover with the cream.
Top with the strawberry halves, brush with the remaining warm glaze and
garnish with mint leaves.

blueberry tart
Prepare the basic recipe, using fresh blueberries in place of the strawberries
and blueberry jam in place of the strawberry jam.

french fruit tart
Prepare the basic recipe, using only a half portion of the glaze and adding
rhubarb to the filling. Cook 500 g (1 lb 2 oz) chopped rhubarb with 225 g (8
oz) raw sugar, 1 teaspoon vanilla essence and 2 tablespoons water until soft;
cool. Spread a very thin layer of glaze over the base of the tart to seal, then
pour the rhubarb into the pie crust. Top with strawberries brushed with the
remaining glaze. Omit the mint leaves.

baked goods

Baking without eggs does represent a challenge, but using a chemistry set of leavening agents and a selection of flours does the trick. The following recipes won't disappoint. The dairy-free fudge is an unexpected treat too!

raisin–walnut quick bread

see variations page 272

Quick breads are perfect for the lunchbox because they are best eaten the day after baking. This recipe uses ground flax seeds and walnuts, both of which are high in omega-3 fatty acids – good news for those avoiding fish oil supplements.

125 g (4 oz) plain flour
2 tsp baking powder
¼ tsp salt
125 g (4 oz) fine wholemeal flour
175 g (6 oz) raisins
175 g (6 oz) soft brown sugar

125 g (4 oz) slivered almonds
1 tsp ground flax seed
4 tbsp water
1 tsp orange rind
125 ml (4 fl oz) freshly squeezed orange juice
125 ml (4 fl oz) sunflower oil

Preheat oven to 180°C (350°F/Gas mark 4). Grease and flour a 23x12-cm (2-pound) loaf tin. In a large bowl, sift together the plain flour, baking powder and salt, then add the wholemeal flour. Toss in the raisins, coating them in flour to prevent them from sticking together and sinking while cooking. Stir in the sugar and almonds and mix thoroughly. In a small bowl, blend together the ground flax seed and water until white and foamy. Add the orange rind orange juice and sunflower oil.

Stir the wet ingredients into the dry ingredients and mix until just blended, adding a little more orange juice or water if the mixture feels stiff; do not overmix. Pour the mixture into the prepared pan and bake for 60 minutes or until the loaf is firm to the touch and a cocktail stick inserted into the centre of the loaf comes out clean. Cool the loaf for 10 minutes before removing from the tin and cooling on a wire rack.

Makes 1 loaf

lemon–poppy seed cupcakes

see variations page 273

These cupcakes are delicious with a cup of tea. They have a bright, zingy taste accentuated by the strong crusty syrup on top. The lemon juice activates the baking soda, which makes these cupcakes rise so successfully and gives them a good texture.

2250 g (9 oz) plain flour
2 tbsp cornflour
1½ tsp bicarbonate of soda
¾ tsp salt
50 g (2 oz) semolina or brown rice flour
4 tbsp poppy seeds
300 ml (½ pt) oat milk or other non-dairy milk

125 g (4 oz) soya margarine, melted
175 ml (6 fl oz) rapeseed or sunflower oil
4 tbsp freshly squeezed lemon juice
rind of 1 small lemon
for the lemon syrup
6 tbsp freshly squeezed lemon juice
65 g (2½ oz) granulated or raw sugar

Preheat oven to 180°C (350°F/Gas mark 4). Line a muffin tin with paper muffin cups. In a bowl, sift together the flour, cornflour, bicarbonate of soda and salt. Stir in the semolina and poppy seeds. Make a well in the middle and pour in the milk, melted margarine, oil and lemon juice. Use a wire whisk to combine. Stir in the lemon rind.

Pour the batter into the prepared baking cases to about 1.5 cm (½ inch) from the top. Bake for 20 to 25 minutes, until a cocktail stick inserted into the centre comes out clean. Meanwhile, stir together the lemon juice and sugar for the topping. When the cupcakes are done, stab them all over with a cocktail stick. Using a teaspoon, drizzle the syrup over the hot cupcakes, letting the syrup soak into them. Remove from the pan and cool on a wire rack.

Makes 12 cupcakes

chocolate brownies

see variations page 274

This brownie recipe is for those who like their brownies strongly chocolaty and soft and gooey in the middle with a slight crustiness on the top. Decadent or what?

75 g (3 oz) soya margarine
75 g (3 oz) plain vegan chocolate
125 g (4 oz) granulated sugar
125 g (4 oz) brown sugar
1 tsp vanilla essence

egg replacer for 2 eggs (page 24)
4 tbsp oat milk or other non-dairy milk
75 g (3 oz) plain flour

Preheat oven to 180°C (350°F/Gas mark 4).

Grease an 20x20-cm (8x8-inch) cake tin and line the base with greaseproof paper. Melt the margarine and chocolate in a bowl placed over a saucepan of simmering water, stirring occasionally. Remove from the heat. Stir in the granulated sugar, brown sugar and vanilla.

In a small bowl, whisk together the egg replacer and the oat milk until frothy. Pour into the chocolate mixture and stir. Sift in the flour and stir until all the ingredients are just combined. Pour the mixture into the prepared tin and bake for about 25 minutes, until the centre of the cake is just firm to touch and has set. Do not overcook; the brownies should be very soft. Allow to cool for 10 minutes, then remove from the pan and cut into pieces.

Makes 9–12 brownies

cranberry–orange oatmeal biscuits

see variations page 275

These are great biscuits, stuffed full of fruit and flavour. The bicarbonate of soda is activated by the hot liquid, so it is best to work quickly to mix it into the batter and not to delay the cooking.

225 g (8 oz) soya margarine
125 g (4 oz) brown sugar
125 g (4 oz) caster sugar
75 g (3 oz) plain flour, sifted
75 g (3 oz) fine wholemeal flour
½ tsp salt

4 tbsp orange juice
1 tsp bicarbonate of soda
grated rind of 1 orange
150 g (5 oz) quick-cooking oats
200 g (7 oz) dried cranberries

Preheat oven to 180°C (350°F/Gas mark 4). Lightly grease 1 or 2 baking trays. In a large bowl, beat the margarine and the sugars until light and fluffy. Stir in the flours and salt. Bring the orange juice to the boil in a small saucepan, remove from the heat and stir in the bicarbonate of soda to dissolve. Quickly add the mixture to the bowl, along with the orange rind, oats and cranberries.

Drop the mixture by teaspoonfuls for small biscuits (or by tablespoonfuls for larger biscuits) onto the baking tray, leaving space between them to allow them to spread. Cook for 10 to 12 minutes, until the edges become a light golden brown. Cool for 3 minutes, then transfer biscuits to a wire rack to cool completely. Repeat until all the mixture is used.

Makes 15–30 cookies

carrot cake with lemon icing

see variations page 276

If you wish, you can use just wholemeal flour and brown sugar, but choose a finely milled wholemeal flour for best effect.

125 g (4 oz) plain flour, sifted
125 g (4 oz) wholemeal flour
4 tbsp cornflour
250 g (8 oz) brown sugar
125 g (4 oz) granulated sugar
1½ tsp ground cinnamon
egg replacer for 2 eggs (page 24)
4 tbsp orange juice
300 ml (10 fl oz) sunflower oil
250 ml (8 oz) soya milk

1 tbsp cider vinegar
350 g (12 oz) grated carrots
75 g (3 oz) sultanas
50 g (2 oz) chopped pecans or walnuts
for the icing
125 g (4 oz) non-dairy cream cheese
50 g (2 oz) soya margarine, melted
1 tsp vanilla essence
1 tsp lemon juice
300 g (10 oz) icing sugar

Preheat oven to 180°C (350°F/Gas mark 4). Grease a 23x33-cm (9x13-inch) cake tin and line the base with greaseproof paper. Combine the flours, cornflour, sugars and cinnamon in a large bowl. In a separate bowl, mix the egg replacer with 2 tablespoons orange juice and whisk until fluffy. Pour into the dry ingredients with remaining orange juice, sunflower oil, soya milk and cider vinegar. Mix, ensuring all dry ingredients are moistened. Stir in carrots, followed by sultanas and nuts. Pour mixture into prepared tin. Bake 40–50 minutes, or until the cake feels firm to touch and a cocktail stick inserted into the centre comes out clean. Cool for 10 minutes before turning out onto a wire rack to cool completely. To make the icing: beat non-dairy cream cheese until soft and smooth, stir in melted margarine, vanilla and lemon juice. Sift in icing sugar until the icing is of spreading consistency. Spread over cake.

Serves 4

banana cake & passion fruit glaze

see variations page 277

Banana cake goes well with the bold taste of passion fruit – vegan cakes needn't be dull!

3 large ripe bananas
4 tbsp sunflower oil
4 tbsp oat milk
125 g (4 oz) brown sugar
1 tbsp rum or 1 tsp vanilla essence
egg replacer for 1 egg (page 24)
1 tbsp water
175 g (6 oz) fine wholemeal flour
1 tsp baking powder

1 tsp salt
¼ tsp ground cinnamon
¼ tsp ground nutmeg
75 g (3 oz) chopped walnuts

for the passion fruit glaze
passion fruit pulp from 4 passion fruit
6 tbsp brown rice syrup or golden syrup
1 tbsp brown sugar

Preheat oven to 180°C (350°F/Gas mark 4). Oil a 20x20-cm (8x8-inch) cake tin. Line the base with greaseproof paper. Mash the bananas and immediately stir in the oil. Stir in the oat milk, brown sugar and rum or vanilla. Whisk the egg replacer and water until frothy. In a separate bowl, combine the flour, baking powder, salt, cinnamon and nutmeg. Pour banana mixture and the egg replacer into the flour mixture and stir until combined, ensuring all dry ingredients are moistened. Add walnuts. Pour the mixture into the prepared tin. Bake for 35–40 minutes until firm to touch and a cocktail stick inserted into the centre comes out clean. Cool for 10 minutes, then turn out and cool completely on a wire rack. For the glaze, combine the passion fruit pulp, syrup, and sugar in a saucepan. Cook over gentle heat until sugar has dissolved. Increase heat, bring to the boil, and cook, without stirring, for about 2 minutes, until it has thickened slightly. Remove from heat. The glaze will continue to thicken as it cools. When the cake and glaze are fully cooled, spread the glaze over the cake.

Serves 8–12

high-energy biscuits

see variations page 278

These biscuits are great for lunchboxes or to take on a hike. If it is going to be a hot day, omit the carob drizzle on the top.

50 g (2 oz) soya margarine
4 tbsp unsweetened apple sauce
175 g (6 oz) brown sugar
90 g (3 oz) crunchy peanut butter
125 g (4 oz) plain flour
1 tsp bicarbonate of soda
$\frac{1}{2}$ tsp salt
egg replacer for 1 egg (page 24)

1 tbsp water
1 tsp vanilla essence
40 g (1$\frac{1}{2}$ oz) quick-cooking oats
175 g (6 oz) mixed dried fruit (raisins and
    chopped apricots, prunes and/or figs)
40 g (1$\frac{1}{2}$ oz) pumpkin seeds
50 g (2 oz) squares vegan semisweet carob bar

Preheat oven to 180°C (350°F/Gas mark 4). Lightly grease 1 or 2 baking trays. In a bowl, beat together the margarine, apple sauce, brown sugar and peanut butter. In a separate bowl, sift together the flour, bicarbonate of soda and salt. In a cup, mix the egg replacer with the water and whisk with a fork until frothy. Stir the dry ingredients and the egg replacer into the margarine mixture. Add the vanilla, oats, dried fruit and pumpkin seeds.

Drop the mixture by tablespoonfuls onto the baking trays, leaving space between them to allow them to spread. Cook for 10 to 12 minutes, until the edges become a light golden brown. Cool for 3 minutes, then transfer to a wire rack. Repeat until all the mixture is used. Once the biscuits are cool, melt the carob and drizzle it on top of the biscuits.

Makes 15–18 cookies

lavender-dusted lemon shortbread

see variations page 279

Lavender sugar is available to purchase, but you can make your own from a small handful of lavender petals sewn into a small cotton pouch. Place this into a jar containing 225 g (8 oz) caster sugar and leave it for 2 weeks, shaking occasionally.

175 g (6 oz) plain flour
50 g (2 oz) cornflour
pinch salt
125 g (4 oz) caster sugar

225 g (8 oz) soya margarine
rind of 1 lemon
2–3 tbsp lavender sugar, to dust

Preheat oven to 150°C (300°FGas mark 2). Lightly grease a baking tray. Place the flour, cornflour and salt into a food processor and pulse a few times to sift and combine. Cut the margarine into chunks and add to the flour with the sugar and lemon rind. Pulse until the fat is fully incorporated. If making the dough without a food processor, rub the margarine into the flour, cornflour and salt; then add the sugar and lemon rind. Turn the mixture out onto a lightly floured work surface and knead together. into a dough. Roll out into a circle about 8 mm (1/3 inch) thick and crimp the edges either with your thumb and forefinger or with a fork. Prick the surface of the shortbread all over with a fork and mark into 8 wedges. Alternatively, press the dough into a 8-cm (1/3-inch) thick rectangle, prick all over and mark into fingers.

Transfer the dough onto the baking tray and bake for about 25 minutes until very lightly golden at the edges. Cool for 5 minutes before cutting into segments and transferring to a wire rack to cool completely. Dust with the lavender sugar.

Makes 8 shortbread biscuits

chocolate cake with glossy icing

see variations page 280

This is such a decadent chocolate cake – even your nonvegan guests will be surprised.

225 g (8 oz) raw or soft brown sugar
75 g (3 oz) white vegetable fat, at room
    temperature
175 g (6 oz) plain flour, sifted or wholemeal flour
4 tbsp cocoa powder
1 tsp bicarbonate of soda
¼ tsp baking powder
½ tsp salt
250 ml (8 fl oz) cold water
1 tbsp cider vinegar

1 tsp vanilla essence
for the icing
40 g (1½ oz) white vegetable fat
75 g (3 oz) vegan plain chocolate
75 ml (3 fl oz) soya milk
1 tsp vanilla essence
¼ tsp salt
275 g (9 oz) icing sugar
chopped pistachio or macadamia nuts,
    to decorate

Preheat oven to 180°C (350°F/Gas mark 4). Grease two 20-cm (8-inch) round pans and line the bases with greaseproof paper. Combine the sugar and white vegetable fat in a bowl or food processor and beat to combine; the mixture will look like crumbs. Add all the remaining ingredients and beat well. Divide the batter between the prepared cake tins and bake for 25 to 35 minutes or until the cakes feel firm to touch and a cocktail stick inserted into the centre comes out clean. Cool for 5 minutes, then turn out onto a wire rack to cool completely. To make the icing, melt the white vegetable fat and chocolate in a bowl placed over a saucepan of simmering water. Stir occasionally. Remove the bowl from the heat and stir in the milk, vanilla and salt. Sift in the icing sugar until the icing is of spreading consistency. Use to sandwich the cakes together, then spread the remainder on top of the cake. Decorate with chopped pistachio or macadamia nuts.

Makes 12 slices

vanilla fudge

see variations page 281

This fudge makes a terrific gift for vegans and anyone on a dairy-free diet. Give it to nonvegans, and they will express surprise. They never thought vegans could have it so good!

375 ml (12 fl oz) soya milk
225 g (8 oz) sugar

125 g (4 oz) soya margarine
2 tsp vanilla essence

Grease a 18x18-cm (7x7-inch) baking tin and line it with greaseproof paper. Place the soya milk, sugar and margarine in a very large pan – the mixture expands considerably while boiling. Insert a sugar thermometer and cook over moderate heat until the sugar has dissolved. Bring to the boil, cover and cook for 3 minutes. Remove the cover and continue to simmer for 15 to 20 minutes, stirring constantly, until a sugar thermometer reaches soft ball stage, 114°C (270°F). (If you do not have a sugar thermometer, drop a little of the mixture into a cup of cold water. It will form into a soft ball when it is hot enough; until then it will just disperse in the water.)

It is extremely important to stir continuously throughout this process, as fudge can easily scorch. Remove the fudge from the heat immediately and place the base of the pan into a bowl of cold water to cool quickly and stop the cooking process. Stir in the vanilla and beat until the mixture thickens and loses its gloss. Pour into the prepared baking tin and place on a wire rack. When almost set, mark into 2.5-cm (1-inch) squares. When it has cooled and set completely, cut into pieces. Arrange in a decorative box or in plastic bags tied with raffia ribbon.

Makes 49 pieces

raisin–walnut quick bread

see base recipe page 257

date–walnut quick bread
Prepare the basic recipe, using chopped dates in place of the raisins.

cranberry–pecan quick bread
Prepare the basic recipe, using dried cranberries in place of the raisins and pecans in place of the walnuts.

cherry–almond quick bread
Prepare the basic recipe, using roughly chopped dried cherries in place of the raisins and flaked almonds in place of the walnuts.

courgette quick bread
Prepare the basic recipe, replacing the raisins with 200 g (7 oz) grated courgette, 1 teaspoon ground cinnamon and ½ teaspoon bicarbonate of soda.

variations

lemon–poppy seed cupcakes

see base recipe page 258

lemon & lime poppy seed cupcakes
Prepare the basic cupcake recipe, using the rind of ½ lemon and ½ lime in place
of the lemon rind. In both the cake and the syrup, use 2 tablespoons lemon juice
and 2 tablespoons lime juice in place of the lemon juice.

orange–poppy seed cupcakes
Prepare the basic cupcake recipe, using 4 tablespoons orange juice and the rind
of half a large orange in place of the lemon juice and rind. In the syrup, use 3
tablespoons orange juice and 1 tablespoon lemon juice.

lemon–almond cupcakes
Prepare the basic recipe, using 40 g (1½ oz) ground almonds in place of the
poppy seeds.

orange–almond cupcakes
Prepare the orange poppy seed cupcakes (above). Additionally, use 40 g (1½ oz)
ground almonds in place of the poppy seeds.

variations

chocolate brownies

see base recipe page 260

hot chocolate brownies
Prepare the basic recipe. Serve as soon as the brownies are cut into pieces, accompanied by chocolate chip vegan or vanilla 'ice cream' (page 239).

chocolate almond brownies
Prepare the basic recipe, adding 50 g (2 oz) slivered almonds and a few drops of almond essence to the batter.

chocolate chip brownies
Prepare the basic recipe, adding to the mixture 75 g (3 oz) vegan plain chocolate, cut into small chunks.

wholemeal chocolate chip brownies
Prepare the basic recipe, using wholemeal flour in place of plain flour and substituting brown sugar for the white sugar. Add 2 extra tablespoons soya milk to the batter.

variations

cranberry-orange oatmeal cookies

see base recipe page 261

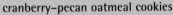

cranberry–pecan oatmeal cookies
Prepare the basic mixture, using 4 tablespoons boiling water in place of the orange juice, 1 teaspoon vanilla essence in place of the orange rind and 125 g (4 oz) chopped pecans and only 125 g (4 oz) dried cranberries.

raisin–pecan oatmeal cookies
Prepare the cranberry and pecan variation above, but use raisins in place of the cranberries.

chocolate chip–orange oatmeal cookies
Prepare the basic recipe, using 225 g (8 oz) chopped vegan plain, milk or white chocolate in place of the cranberries.

blueberry–orange oatmeal cookies
Prepare the basic recipe, using 175 g (6 oz) fresh blueberries in place of the dried cranberries. (Blueberries work well in the cranberry pecan oat variation too, using 75 g (3 oz) blueberries in place of the cranberries.)

carrot cake with lemon icing

see base recipe page 262

carrot & pineapple cake with lemon icing
Prepare the basic recipe, replacing half the shredded carrots 225 g (8 oz) well-drained tinned crushed pineapple.

carrot & courgette cake with lemon icing
Prepare the basic recipe, replacing half the shredded carrots with 150 g (5 oz) shredded courgette.

carrot cake with passion fruit glaze
Prepare the basic carrot cake, but replace the icing with a double quantity of passion fruit glaze (page 265).

carrot cake with lemon-coconut icing
Prepare the basic recipe. Lightly toast 65 g (2½ oz) shredded coconut under a medium-hot grill until the edges become lightly golden – watch carefully as it quickly burns. Cool and lightly press into the icing.

banana cake & passion fruit glaze

see base recipe page 265

banana cake & chocolate chips
Prepare the basic recipe, using 125 g (4 oz) chopped vegan plain chocolate
in place of the walnuts. Sprinkle 2 tablespoons brown sugar (a crystalline
sugar such as Demerara is good) over the top of the cake before baking.
Omit the glaze.

banana & orange cake with passion fruit glaze
Prepare the basic recipe, using 2 tablespoons orange juice, the rind of 1 orange
and 1 teaspoon lemon juice in place of the rum or vanilla essence.

banana raisin cake & passion fruit glaze
Prepare the basic recipe, adding 125 g (4 oz) raisins to the batter.

banana almond cake & passion fruit glaze
Prepare the basic recipe, replacing 25 g (1 oz) of the wholemeal flour with 25 g
(1 oz) ground almonds. Also, use 75 g (3 oz) chopped blanched almonds in place
of the walnuts.

high-energy biscuits

see base recipe page 266

gluten-free high-energy biscuits
Prepare the basic recipe, using gluten-free flour in place of the plain flour.
Add 1–2 tablespoons soya milk to the mixture if it feels stiff (gluten-free
flours tend to be drier than wheat flours).

carob high-energy biscuits
Prepare the basic recipe, using only 125 g (4 oz) mixed fruit and adding 50 g
(2 oz) chopped vegan carob bar to the mixture.

granola carob biscuits
Prepare the basic recipe, using 175 g (6 oz) granola and 50 g (2 oz) chopped
vegan carob bar in place of the oats, mixed fruit and pumpkin seeds.

almond apricot high-energy biscuits
Prepare the basic recipe, using almond butter in place of the peanut butter.
Using chopped dried apricots in place of the mixed fruit and 50 g (2 oz)
chopped blanched almonds in place of the pumpkin seeds.

variations

lavender-dusted lemon shortbread

see base recipe page 267

traditional scottish shortbread
Prepare the basic recipe, using 125 g (4 oz) plain flour plus 60 g (2 oz) rice flour and omitting the lemon rind. Dust with caster sugar instead of lavender sugar.

ginger shortbread
Prepare the basic recipe, using 4 tablespoons finely chopped stem ginger in place of the lemon rind. Dust with caster sugar instead of lavender sugar.

lavender-dusted pecan shortbread
Prepare the basic recipe, using 50 g (2 oz) finely chopped pecans in place of the lemon rind.

chocolate chip shortbread
Prepare the basic recipe, using 50 g (2 oz) finely chopped vegan plain or milk chocolate in place of the lemon rind. There is no need to dust these cookies with additional sugar after cooking.

chocolate cake with glossy icing

see base recipe page 268

carob cake with glossy icing
Prepare the basic recipe, using carob powder in place of the cocoa powder in the cake. Use carob in place of chocolate in the icing.

mocha cake with glossy icing
Prepare the basic recipe, using 2 teaspoons instant coffee with the cocoa. Add 1 teaspoon instant coffee to the icing.

chocolate cupcakes
Prepare the basic recipe. Pour the batter into paper liners in a muffin tin. Fill to about 1 cm (½ inch) from the top of the liners, then bake for 20 to 25 minutes until a cocktail stick inserted into the cupcake centres comes out clean. Cool, then use the icing to decorate the individual cupcakes.

chocolate sponge pudding
Prepare a half portion of the basic cake recipe and bake it in a 18-cm (7-inch) ovenproof dish that has been greased and lined with greaseproof paper. Allow to cool for 5 minutes, turn out onto a plate and serve hot with vanilla vegan 'ice cream' (page 239). Omit the icing.

vanilla fudge

see base recipe page 271

chocolate fudge
Prepare the basic recipe, using just 1 teaspoon vanilla essence. Stir the vanilla and 100 g (3½ oz) vegan plain chocolate into the mixture at the same time.

mocha fudge
Prepare the chocolate fudge variation above, but use 2 teaspoons instant coffee in place of the 2 teaspoons vanilla essence.

vanilla cherry fudge
Prepare the basic recipe, stirring in 50 g (2 oz) chopped glacé cherries to the mixture at the same time as the vanilla.

rum raisin fudge
Prepare the basic recipe, using 50 g (2 oz) plump raisins and 2 tablespoons rum in place of the vanilla.

nutty almond fudge
Prepare the basic recipe, using 50 g (2 oz) roughly chopped toasted almonds and a few drops of almond essence in place of the vanilla.

index

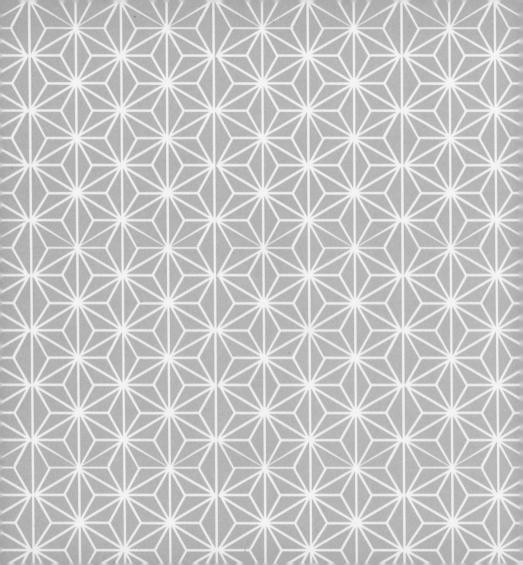